PRAISE FOR AUSTRALIA 2034

"In its short history, Australia has shown remarkable resilience to changing circumstances. However, unless our leaders wake up to the challenges of today's rapidly evolving business environment, our prized status as 'the lucky country' is threatened.

Nigel Andrade and Peter Munro's book calls out some uncomfortable truths and provides valuable perspectives on seven core capabilities that all business leaders and their boards should be carefully considering when developing their business strategies.

Any business leader intent on creating a successful organization will benefit from this thoughtful and challenging book. The authors blend stories and theory as they provide a summary of the leadership mindset and critical capabilities that need to be embraced now in order to position businesses for success—today and in the future."

David Cartwright, Non-Executive Director, Super Partners and Non-Executive Director, Melbourne Health

"Business planning is never easy but planning 20 years ahead is more art than science. This is particularly the case given the rapidly changing world we now live in. While difficult, the statistics contained in *Australia 2034: Luckier by Design* reinforce the value of long-term planning for all businesses that desire longevity. Of the top 100 Australian companies in the ASX in 1994, only 29 were still part of the Index in 2013. The survival rate in other countries is no better.

While this book is mainly aimed at Australian businesses, the messages are relevant for businesses everywhere. Following the global economic crisis, the world is still struggling to find stable growth and after 20 years of growth, Australia is now facing a similar challenge. The message from A. T. Kearney is that more of the same will not be enough. For long-term success the key messages of the book are clear: Asia matters, but to succeed Australian businesses must be clear on their value propositions and recognize that Asia is not a monolith; it is 27 very different countries with very different cultures. Successful businesses will be those that understand the concept of shared value creation, notably, that there is a direct correlation between a company's success and the health of its related communities (including suppliers, customers, employees, and shareholders).

A focus on value will be particularly important with respect to the customer. Tomorrow's customer will expect products and services that are relevant for their lifestyles. Achieving these outcomes will require a very different approach to business management. Organizations that succeed will understand that change is a constant. This means that businesses have to be agile, with a focus on continuous improvement, including a passion for productivity through a culture of continuous improvement. Analytics will be essential to ensure that the customer and organizational dynamics are understood and that the organization is able to respond appropriately.

In summary, this is not a world where businesses can stand still. The authors provide case studies of companies that have both failed and succeeded to recognize the shifts around them and the follow-on consequences. For all those business leaders who recognize the challenges ahead but struggle to know where to begin, this book provides a practical approach to success. The book concludes: 'the future will be inherently uncertain, therefore businesses need to arm themselves with the necessary capabilities to navigate in an uncertain world'. Reading this book is an essential first step towards a more certain future."

Anne Weatherston, Former CIO and Management Board Member, ANZ Bank

"*Australia 2034: Luckier by Design* is a compelling read for the managers of today and tomorrow. Andrade and Munro leave no stone unturned in forcing the reader to agree that the old methods of business management are not robust or inclusive enough in a globalizing world. They argue that shareholder value creation (SVC) comes from benefitting communities not just individuals and give detailed evidence to support this approach. The authors supply a set of systems, processes, and measures that can be adapted to any business to deliver SVC.

Andrade and Munro lead us through the key attributes required of businesses that are to survive through to 2034. Businesses should lead through value innovation. Innovation requires agility and this agility needs to be in the DNA of the business—that is, it needs to be represented in all phases of the business, from planning through to delivery. Andrade and Munro show us that agile organizations have a purpose, are fit to compete, and have a level of diversity to ameliorate risk. In this way, they can manage their way through the disruption that organizations and businesses inevitably encounter. This disruption is caused by the inherent conflict between market share and profitability. Fit organizations confront disruption before it occurs.

The authors then lead us through the concept of value innovation, focusing on how organizations create value for customers. The concept of customer-centric marketing has been around for some time. Andrade and Munro take this concept and show us that in many cases this is not what the customer truly needs. Pivotal Customer Events should be identified and strategies deployed to take advantage of these events. Rightfully, Andrade and Munro argue that 'reliable and continuous creation of customer value will be crucial and a lasting source of strategic advantage'. This section also focuses on productivity. While many organizations confuse productivity with cost reduction, the authors contend that true productivity requires a focus on both outputs and inputs to create sustainable value.

Andrade and Munro have produced an important piece of work that should be read closely and that leaves the reader accepting that success is better from design than from just pure luck. This design requires a new way of thinking and delivery if we are to be as successful in the future as we have been in the past."

Peter Gregg, Former CFO, Leighton Holdings and Qantas Airways

"Nigel Andrade and Peter Munro have authored a highly credible book which captures and articulates many of the key forces at play in recognizing, responding to, and succeeding in Australian investment in Asia. They are generous in offering 20 years of grace for the changing Asian landscape to provide opportunities—as one can see the pace of change rapidly unfolding—with the lag from the developed world continuously shortening. The onset of digital is further shortening this lag.

Across many individual markets of Asia, foreign strategic investors are taking up key market positions. Thus, Australian business is not only in competition with its own ability to mobilize, but also with the rest of the developed world that is moving increasingly faster.

Growing market size and lack of available positions will over time make feasible investment out of reach for many of today's potential investors. Living and working in Asia for just on 10 years has taught me many important things about success in the region. Most notably, Asia is more a challenge of resilience, cultural adaptation, and an appreciation that what Australian and Western-based businesses value as a strong commercial basis for business can be very different from what their Asian partners value. Asian businesses place more weight on who you are, what your reputation is, how you conduct yourself, and how you are perceived by others; there is much more emphasis on the 'who' rather than the 'what'. Further, as partnership models form the majority of business interactions given FDI regulation, often the potential to gain advantage and control in the investment is the ability to identify the best points of leverage across the business and work on those, rather than aspiring to conquer everything.

The authors rightly identify 'Asia is not for everyone', and thus to deal with the ambiguity, operational risk, and underdeveloped nature of controls and market environments, investors must not rely on the familiarity and robustness associated with their home market systems. Rather, they must see themselves as part of the longer term solution and vehicle to raise standards and capabilities that will lift Asian markets to international standards, deliver value for all stakeholders, and ultimately crystallize as reality a truly shared value."

Duncan Brain, Asia Pacific CEO, IAG

AUS
TRA
LIA
2034

LUCKIER
BY DESIGN

LID Publishing Ltd
Garden Studios, 71-75 Shelton Street
Covent Garden, London WC2H 9JQ

31 West 34th Street, Suite 7004,
New York, NY 10001, US

info@lidpublishing.com
www.lidpublishing.com

A member of:

BPR
Business Publishers Roundtable

www.businesspublishersroundtable.com

Printed and bound by CPI Group (UK) Ltd, Croydon CR0 4YY

ISBN: 978-1-907794-97-1

Cover and page design: Laura Hawkins

AUS TRA LIA 2034

LUCKIER BY DESIGN

NIGEL P ANDRADE
PETER D MUNRO

LONDON   MONTERREY
MADRID   SHANGHAI
MEXICO CITY   BOGOTA
NEW YORK   BUENOS AIRES
BARCELONA   SAN FRANCISCO

TABLE OF CONTENTS

FOREWORD

I start by complimenting A.T. Kearney, first for what they have achieved in Australia since their formation here two decades ago, and second for choosing to give Australia this book, *Australia 2034: Luckier by Design* in celebration of their 20th anniversary.

I am on record as lamenting how we in Australia, in most facets and sectors, tend to think more short term than our neighbours in Southeast Asia. I fervently believe that short-term thinking will put us ultimately at a competitive disadvantage. We urgently need to realise that for the sake of our children, our businesses, and our country generally we must look out further and contemplate a longer-term perspective.

The essence of this book encourages thinking beyond the short term and posits where Australia will be heading over the next 20 years. It starts by looking at what's happened over the last two decades and seeks to project the relevant trends forward. The authors set out a number of capability sets, which to me make sense, and conclude above all that whilst it is impossible to predict the future, one has to prepare for it.

"Luckier by Design" is a much more fitting epithet for the next 20 years than the "Lucky Country" or indeed the "Clever Country". I commend all those involved in this book and sincerely hope that it will be read, analysed, and acted upon.

David Gonski AC

PART I:
INTRODUCTION

This year marks the 20th anniversary of A.T. Kearney in Australia. Since 1994, we have had the privilege to occupy front-row seats and participate in the changes that have shaped our vibrant and successful economy. Our team has spent the past year reflecting on these shifts and thinking about what the future might have in store for us. We've concluded that Australian businesses will need bigger ambitions and unprecedented capabilities to build on the successes of the past two decades and realise their full potential over the next two.

In short, companies need to embrace what we call a 2034 Capability Manifesto for Australian Business:

- **Nurture a more expansive mindset**. Think beyond our traditional boundaries to discover opportunities from actively engaging with Asia and placing shared social and environmental value at the centre of economic activities
- **Inject agility into our DNA**. Think and behave with foresight, speed, and decisiveness to lead in an increasingly volatile and uncertain world
- **Lead through "value innovation"**. Create customer value, recognise productivity as a strategy, and use analytics to fundamentally increase competitiveness and reach world-class performance levels.

To appreciate the pace of change, we only need to consider how the world around us has transformed in the short space of two decades. We don't have a crystal ball and will not attempt to predict the future, but we do assert that we can shape our fortunes based on how we choose to prepare and respond to the key demographic, political, social, and technological trends we face.

Against this backdrop, we wrote *Australia 2034: Luckier by Design*. The book presents our perspective on the capabilities that will make Australia and Australian businesses a force to reckon with on the global stage and to collectively raise our aspirations as a country—to be known not only as the "Lucky Country", whether used ironically or not, but instead as the country that is "Luckier by Design".

CHAPTER 1

LOOKING BACK, LOOKING AHEAD

Over the past 20 years, Australia has written one of the most remarkable economic growth stories of the century. Australia today is much stronger than it was just 20 short years ago. In many respects, we've been fortunate. The country is blessed with abundant mineral resources that are (and will remain) in heavy demand as Asia continues to urbanise and industrialise. Terms of trade have evolved strongly in our favour. The country's tolerant atmosphere, high educational and healthcare standards, secure legal environment, and wealth of job opportunities have made it a magnet for talented and ambitious people from around the region seeking a better life. And its people have shown resilience time and again in the face of adversity, as the country quickly bounces back from recurring natural disasters such as droughts, floods, and bushfires.

Although the plot started much earlier, the window between 1994 and 2014 has seen several fundamental, largely positive shifts in the country's economy, people, and business. In these past two decades, Australia has come into its own in the world—expanding demographically, economically, and politically. Australians have grown slightly older on average, increased their net worth, and become better connected with the rest of the world. Australian businesses, meanwhile, have flourished in number and profitability.

Looking forward, however, the outlook is less certain. Change is bearing down on us at a record pace. Asia is developing very rapidly, taking on an ever stronger economic and political role in the region. Technology changes are reaching into all facets of life and shaping a wide range of social behaviours and business practices. Migration and an ageing population will continue to shape our country. And a wide range of social pressures, from environmental concerns to increasing religious and social activism, will need to be addressed.

Our luck could continue—or it might run out, depending on how we choose to navigate this next period of our economic history.

In this chapter, we look back, briefly analysing the road Australia has travelled since 1994; we look forward to better understand the challenges and opportunities that lie ahead; and we propose a manifesto of capabilities that Australian businesses will need to cultivate to successfully navigate the next 20 years.

LOOKING BACK 20 YEARS

Australia has come a long way as a nation (see figure 1). Compared to most other markets, both developed and emerging, we have seen an almost unbroken trend towards increasing prosperity.

FIGURE 1: NONSTOP PROGRESS TOWARDS NATIONAL PROSPERITY
Australian economy: 1994 vs. today

LARGER, RICHER, MORE URBANISED POPULATION

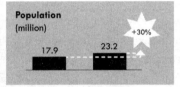

Population (million)
+30%
17.9   23.2

More people
due to increased immigration, mainly to the major cities

SHIFTING ECONOMIC MIX

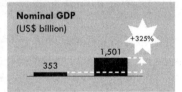

Nominal GDP (US$ billion)
+325%
353   1,501

GDP growth
influenced by shift in economic mix towards high-value industries (such as retail, finance, and mining)

GREATER ASIAN INFLUENCE

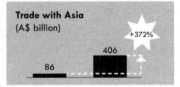

Trade with Asia (A$ billion)
+372%
86   406

Increased trade
with Asia, mainly due to more demand and closer cultural ties with Asia

INCREASINGLY POLARISED DEVELOPMENT

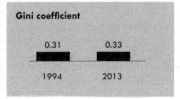

Gini coefficient
0.31   0.33
1994   2013

More income
inequality caused by technological shift that places premium on highly skilled workers

Sources: EIU, Australian Bureau of Statistics, OECD; A.T. Kearney analysis

AUSTRALIA: BIGGER, WEALTHIER, AND MORE RELEVANT

Nominal GDP has grown to US$1.5 trillion and per capita income has skyrocketed to US$65,000.[1] Even discounting for inflation, GDP has increased by an amazing 85 per cent over 1994. Twenty years ago, with a population of nearly 18 million and a GDP of more than US$350 billion, Australia's GDP per capita was around US$20,000, according to the Economist Intelligence Unit. Agriculture and manufacturing were the main growth engines, although the move towards services was well underway. The country was a net importer of goods and services, and our three largest trading partners—Japan, the United States, and the United Kingdom—accounted for more than 40 per cent of total trade. Today, services and primary materials are the new growth engines. Australia is still a net importer, but trade—particularly with Asia—has blossomed. China is now our biggest commercial partner, generating more than 20 per cent of our trade in goods and services, followed by the United States and Japan. Our centre of gravity has shifted eastward, as trade volume with Asia is now quadruple that with Europe.[2]

Our personal capital base has also grown substantially. Compulsory superannuation had only just begun as a bold, large-scale economic experiment, but by 1994 we had already built up a capital base of $171 billion (US$133 billion at then-prevailing exchange rates). Today that figure is $1.7 trillion (US$1.5 trillion), equivalent to 100 per cent of our GDP.[3]

Our financial success has run in parallel with the rise in our global standing. Today, we're a member of the G20, a key ally of the United States and NATO, and a non-permanent member of the United Nations Security Council.

It's also worth noting, however, that we are perhaps less egalitarian today than we were 20 years ago. The richest 10 per cent of our population gained a disproportionately high part of the growth in income over the past decades, widening inequality and raising our Gini coefficient from 0.31 to 0.33.[4] Despite a decline in violent and property crimes, imprisonment rates have increased from 139 prisoners per 100,000 inhabitants in 1997 to 170 in 2013.[5]

As we bask in our recent history and look ahead at the next 20 years, we will consider a range of questions that Australian businesses are asking:

• How can we continue to contribute to increased economic prosperity? How can we do so in a socially and environmentally responsible manner?

• How can we help Australia retain its political and economic relevance in a region brimming with rising stars?

• What sectors and distinct capabilities will we pioneer to balance the dependence on primary industries and drive the next wave of value creation?

AUSTRALIANS: MORE MATURE, MORE PROSPEROUS, AND BETTER CONNECTED

Over the past 20 years, Smith has remained the most common surname in Australia. Nonetheless, there are a few key differences between John (the most common first name in 1994) and David (the most common given name in 2014).

John Smith, the average Australian in 1994, earned about A$58,000 a year; his wife Sarah earned less—about A$46,000. He was 33 years old and had married six years ago, eight years after moving out of his parents' house at the tender age of 19. He spent more on meals than on his home, did not own shares, and contributed just 3 per cent of his salary to superannuation. He did not yet own a mobile phone or have Internet access. But, as a forward-thinking young man, he was contemplating buying a computer in the next couple of years.[6]

Fast forward and David Smith, the average Australian of 2014, has aged. He's 38 years old and has only been married for eight years, so he tied the knot when he was three years older than his 1994 counterpart. It was expensive for David to strike out on his own, so he waited until he turned 26 before he left the nest. David works in sales and earns around A$80,000 (in constant 1994 dollars), a one-third increase over John's salary. However, he now spends more on housing than he does on meals (but less than John did on alcohol). To guard against the increasing cost of living, David has invested in shares and puts 9.25 per cent of his salary aside for superannuation. Of course, David owns a mobile phone (with 33 apps, more than people from most other countries), has two computers, and enjoys broadband Internet access at home.[7]

One key nuance that's missing from this story is the tale of our increasing diversity. Today, 30 per cent of Australians are born to non-Australian parents, many of whom are from Lebanon, China, India, and Vietnam rather than Europe. Nguyen, a Vietnamese surname, is the second most common family name today in Melbourne and the third most common in Sydney.[8] Perhaps the Smiths will find themselves knocked off the top spot of the podium 20 years from now.

Australia clearly provides well for its citizens and is attractive for immigrants. It is also true that much still can be done to make life more affordable, prepare today's youth and workforce for the next 20 years, and develop our unique multicultural society.

As leaders of Australian companies ponder the next 20 years, they are likely to ask themselves questions such as:

• What are the business implications of a more diverse talent pool and customer base? How can a more diverse workforce help companies better compete?

- How will a maturing society affect the nature of products and services that are demanded? How will digital breakthroughs affect distribution models and alter value chains?

- What are Australian investors looking for, and how can businesses ensure continued access to the country's growing savings base?

AUSTRALIAN BUSINESSES: MORE NUMEROUS AND PROFITABLE

Australian business has been a linchpin of our prosperity as a nation and a people. Over the past 20 years, Australian businesses have also become stronger (see figure 2).

The average business in 1994 was as likely to be engaged in manufacturing as in retail trade. Its turnover was around $1.6 million a year, its profit margin a healthy 8.3 per cent, and it was predominantly equity financed, with a debt-to-equity ratio of 0.8. Furthermore, its interest coverage ratio—a measure of a company's ability to service its debt—sat at 2.7.[9]

Come 2014, the average business is now a retailer, one of 2 million small and midsize enterprises (a number that has doubled since 1994). Turnover is lower, at $1.2 million (in constant 1994 dollars), but margins have risen to 11 per cent and the interest coverage ratio has improved markedly to 5.0. Moreover, the business has a more diverse and flexible workplace, with a larger proportion of part-time staff.[10]

Sectors such as mining and financial services account for a greater share of GDP, while the relative contribution of the manufacturing sector has declined. In the early 1990s, the commonly accepted notion that Australia's economy needed to be competitive domestically if it was to compete internationally led to the introduction of the National Competition Policy. The new policies, together with related reforms, are estimated to have boosted Australia's GDP by an incremental 2.5 per cent between 1990 and 2000.[11]

However, although businesses as a whole have thrived, some companies have faced wrenching challenges. Only one-third of the companies in the ASX 100 in 1994 are still in the index today. And of the ASX 100 companies in 2014, one-third of them didn't even exist in 1994.

With these shifts in mind, Australian business leaders are working through questions such as:

- What must be done to remain competitive as regional blocs consolidate and global economic integration advances? How important is internationalisation?

FIGURE 2: PROLIFERATION OF BUSINESSES
WITH UNPRECEDENTED RETURNS
Evolution of Australian business since 1994

EXPLOSIVE GROWTH OF SMALL BUSINESSES	STEADILY RISING PROFITABILITY	CHANGING INDUSTRY MIX
• Doubling in number of businesses to nearly 2.2 million, with the vast majority being small enterprises	• Profitability up from 8.3% to 11.1% due to growth in high-margin sectors • Focus on bottom-line growth	• Rise in services such as IT, telecom, finance, resource-led services, and education • Decline in manufacturing

INCREASINGLY DIVERSE AND FLEXIBLE WORKFORCE	GRADUALLY INCREASING PRODUCTIVITY	INCREASED COMPETITION
• Rise of female workers from 42.2% to 46% of total workforce • Increase in part-time workers from 16% to 24.7%	• Shift from low to high value-add industries • Value-add per hour up from A$26 to more than A$53	• Trends towards privatisation, corporatisation, and deregulation • Proliferation followed by consolidation

Sources: Australian Bureau of Statistics, OECD; A.T. Kearney analysis

- How can businesses respond to industry changes and stay one or two steps ahead of the market? How can they remain agile, despite increasing business complexity, and avoid drifting into irrelevance?
- How can a company continue to add value to win against competitors, better serving customers and providing superior shareholder returns?

THE DOUBLE-EDGED SWORD OF DESTINY

With the global financial crisis behind us and the slowdown of the resources boom underway, we often hear that "Australia is at a crossroads". In Australia, as is the case around the world, businesses face significant changes and each one is a double-edged sword. Rather than try to predict our future destiny in what is intrinsically an unpredictable world, we look at key trends to understand what is unfolding around us while recognising that our destiny will depend on how we respond—with the right outlook, capabilities, and strategies—and as such remains very much within our control. Scanning through the copious volumes of literature on trends, we've settled on four megatrends that we believe will have the deepest impact on us over the next two decades (see figure 3).

ASIA RISING

The next century will be defined by Asia. Asia's share of global output has already increased from 18 per cent to 35 per cent over the past 60 years, and it will continue to be one of the world's fastest growing regions. As of mid-2014, the International Monetary Fund (IMF) expects real GDP for emerging and developing Asia to grow by more than 6.4 per cent per annum at least until the next decade—a growth rate of almost three times that of advanced economies, and two times that of Australia.[12]

The breadth and depth of our relationship with Asia will continue to expand in the coming decades. And indeed, this is already occurring at three distinct levels:

- **People.** The face of Australia's immigrant population is shifting from Europe to Asia: today, 2 out of the 5 million overseas-born Australians were born in Asia. Compare this to 1981, when immigrants were primarily European and the Asian immigrant population was only 276,000. Over the past decade alone, Asian migration has grown 12 per cent annually, with China and India being major contributors to this growth.[13] The movement between Asia and Australia is a two-way street: 40 per cent of Australian emigrants are now moving to Asia, and this is expected to increase as economic opportunities increase in the region.[14] The growing Asia-fluent "Australian" workforce in both Australia and Asia has the potential to shift our ability to engage with Asia and extend our influence across cultural and regional boundaries.
- **Trade.** Trade with key Asian economies has grown at 18 per cent annually over the past decade, to US$250 billion.[15] Up until now, the majority of trade with Asian countries has been resource focused; there is still significant opportunity to export our ideas, innovation, and services. We have a sophisticated skills and services sector with capabilities and assets that are heavily demanded in many developing Asian nations. Yet only 15 per cent of our exports are in services, while services sectors such as healthcare and financial services account for more than 50 per cent of our GDP.[16]

FIGURE 3: THE DOUBLE-EDGED SWORD OF DESTINY

MEGATREND	OPPORTUNITIES	THREATS
 ASIA RISING	• Export growth beyond resources • Local market growth due to temporary and permanent immigration • Access to capital; seeking attractive returns in low-risk environment	• Increased rivalry among local businesses • Flood of low-cost imports • Competition for local capital
 MATURING AUSTRALIA	• Rising affluence • Capital accumulation • More time for community and leisure	• Increased healthcare costs • Lower demographic dividend • Investor strategies become overly conservative
 DIGITAL TSUNAMI	• Increased efficiency • Customer value multiplier • New market opportunities	• Fewer intermediaries • Value chain reconfiguration • Erosion of economic surplus and more volatility • Misinformation, security, and privacy
 INCREASED IMBALANCE	• Demand for new energy, resource, and social solutions (domestic and regional) • Ability to play significant leadership role in region	• Frustration with "big business" forces new policies • Loss of moral capital through inaction

Source: A.T. Kearney analysis

- **Capital.** Australia is an attractive investment destination, with Australian businesses offering an appealing return on risk. Incoming investment from Asia has grown steadily, reaching US$20 billion in 2011 (a 50 per cent increase over the past 10 years).[17] At the same time, Asia attracts approximately one-third of all global FDI and remains a top destination for international investors, with China ranking number 2 and India ranking number 7, according to A.T. Kearney's FDI Confidence Index®, 2014.[18] Within this context, the potential for Australia to be an exporter of capital to the region in a world challenged by cautious capital can be significant.

Of course, the rapid development of the Asia region can also be viewed as a threat. Closer Asian integration could intensify domestic competition from lower-cost new entrants, as less expensive imports flood the market and leaner business models gain ascendancy. A growing migrant segment drives changes in customer habits and preferences that may catch Australian businesses off guard. And finally, the availability of attractive investment options in Asia could raise the cost of capital for Australian businesses and capital projects, given the need to compete with other viable investment destinations.

The debate on the Asia Century is intensifying. Actively addressing these questions will be an imperative for all Australian businesses.

MATURING AUSTRALIA

The trend of our ageing population is well established. The average age of Australians has been increasing at a rate of 0.25 years per annum. By 2026, Australia's median age will have risen by another two to four years.

The impact of a more mature population will be significant—on workforce composition, markets, social dynamics, and politics. As Australians get older they get richer and save more, but also have more time for community and leisure activities. The average net worth per capita in real terms has risen from $500,000 to $700,000 in the past 10 years, meaning that there will be vast amounts of capital available for investment. This investment will be crucial to building the economy of the future, provided that investors' strategies do not become overly conservative.

However, there are also obstacles to increasing maturity. Funding a large, post-retirement generation can get expensive as the cost of living takes off and medical costs spiral upward, fuelled by a population living for years with one or more chronic diseases. In a worst-case scenario, balances (though higher) might still be insufficient to cover costs. Further, with the greying of the population, overall GDP could fall if productivity increases fail to offset the disappearing demographic dividend. And, in fact, the country already registered in 2012 a slight downtick in the labour force participation rate.

An ageing population also requires us to rethink how we design products, marketing communications, and retail formats to be more user-friendly to this growing segment, as outlined in A.T. Kearney's study, "What Do Mature Consumers Want?"[19] The way we think about career paths will also be affected, particularly if we are looking to keep an older generation in the economic and social mainstream and take advantage of their know-how to design and provide goods and services to their age group.

DIGITAL TSUNAMI

It's nearly impossible to turn on the news or read a journal without hearing about the rapid and fundamental impact digital technologies are having on the world. By 2016, online retail sales in Australia are forecast to reach $27 billion—an increase of 14 per cent in just two years. The number of Internet-enabled mobile handsets is estimated to have tripled between 2013 and 2014 to around 9 million. Rollout of the National Broadband Network (NBN) is likely to accelerate these trends, with broadband penetration expected to reach 93 per cent by 2019. If the current pattern continues, per capita mobile data consumption will increase from 0.9 GB today to 4.2 GB per month in 2018.

Online connectivity is only the tip of the iceberg. For most countries around the world, the past 20 years have been about putting the connectivity infrastructure in place. In the past 10 years, following the rapid adoption of smartphones and tablets and pioneering efforts by start-ups, new usage behaviours have become established to access information, collaborate with others, share (not just ideas, but also assets such as homes, cars, and equipment), and network socially. The next 20 years will see the widespread application of digital technologies deep into existing businesses and across value chains.

Advances in technology, analytical power, and the "Internet of Things" are picking up the pace in Australia and around the globe. Several industries, such as news and information, entertainment, and travel, have already faced significant disruption and more are likely to follow. Digitisation clearly presents many benefits. First, it allows for greater efficiency and productivity in many areas, from automation to transparency to simplicity in individual and business transactions. It also supports new value propositions as customer experiences are enhanced through the convergence of the physical and virtual worlds. Through this process, customer value is maximised, and faster, better, cheaper products and services will become available. Local businesses will also improve their access to the global marketplace as the online purchase and sale of goods and services becomes second nature.

Yet digitisation also threatens current models. There is the threat of industry disruption and new competitors providing better service and different business models. Also, if unmanaged, digitisation can erode economic surplus and drive volatility higher as it intensifies the pace of change. Finally, it can expose society to risks we are just beginning to understand such as misinformation, fraud, and identity theft, to name a few.

The speed and ingenuity with which Australian businesses embrace digital and other technological advances will be critical not only to defend against changing competitive and market conditions, but also as an opportunity to break new ground to support accelerated growth in Australia and overseas.

INCREASED IMBALANCE

Within Australia and across Asia Pacific, longstanding problems—resource shortages, environmental issues, social and economic inequality, and unemployment—are becoming more acute. The rise of the Asian middle class and increasing affluence in Australia are positive in many ways, but they also place deep strains on our current system.

If every new member of the Asian middle class were to aspire to live the life of the average Australian, we would burn through the planet's resources at astonishing speed. What's more, the gap between the haves and have-nots would widen, with the latter bearing a disproportionate burden of environmental costs.

The shift to digital will increase productivity, but it will also require retraining to acquire new skills that are relevant in an increasingly dynamic world. And while the risks are well understood, progress is slow. Business can no longer afford to be a mere bystander; it will either have to be part of the solution or accept that it is part of the problem. Business's moral capital will slowly erode if it chooses inaction or, worse, short-term profit at all costs.

But this megatrend also brings opportunities. Each of these problems represents a business prospect in some form. For example, demand for food and agriculture, water solutions, clean energy, and waste reduction all present a chance to create value. Indeed, the entire world is looking for answers to these challenges, and Australia has the potential to fill a regional leadership vacuum and show other countries the way towards a more sustainable future.

On the flipside, not addressing the growing resource and social imbalance is likely to lead to increasing regulatory intervention, social activism, or even a market shift away from companies that are slow to respond.

So, in summary, looking at these four megatrends in aggregate, the only thing we know for sure is that the future will be very different from the past. The opportunity for businesses to create value will be transformed as value takes different forms and occurs in different places. We call this phenomenon "value migration". Some will shrink and others will grow leading to "value disruption". And finally, value will be more difficult to acquire as market expectations continue to rise—a condition we refer to as "value commoditisation".

Given the difficulty, if not impossibility, of picking the specific aspects of each trend to prepare for and respond to, the key to winning in the future rests on the capabilities a business chooses to invest in and build. In the next section, we outline our views of the non-negotiable, must-have capabilities that Australian business requires to thrive on the sharp end of the double-edged sword of destiny.

A CAPABILITY MANIFESTO FOR THE NEXT 20 YEARS

Shaping a new Australia and catering to the demands of new Australians amidst these discontinuities are challenges incumbent upon our nation's business community.

Given the strengths our companies have built up over the past two decades, as well as the nature of the opportunities before us over the next two, we can attempt to discover how much time our current aspirations and capabilities will buy us. Or we can embrace a bolder vision for Australian business that will allow us to survive in what Kevin Roberts calls a VUCA world: volatile, uncertain, complex, and ambiguous.[20]

For us, the choice is clear. If Australian businesses are to continue to flourish they must develop three capability sets, which we call the Capability Manifesto: an expansive mindset, an agile DNA, and the ability to deliver new and more innovative value (see figure 4).

CAPABILITY SET 1: NURTURE AN EXPANSIVE MINDSET

An expansive mindset encompasses the ability to understand and imagine where value will be found as it migrates across a broadening economic landscape. A blinkered view of the sources and definition of value is a sure recipe for less relevance.

After 20 years of economic growth, the challenge is that many companies have not tested and honed their ability to constantly explore new value-creating opportunities. We need to learn this skill once again, as it will unlock new horizons of possibilities for Australian business.

By its very nature, an expansive mindset comprises boundless opportunities. Based on the megatrends, two stand out: engaging with Asia (new markets) and unlocking shared value (broad value propositions).

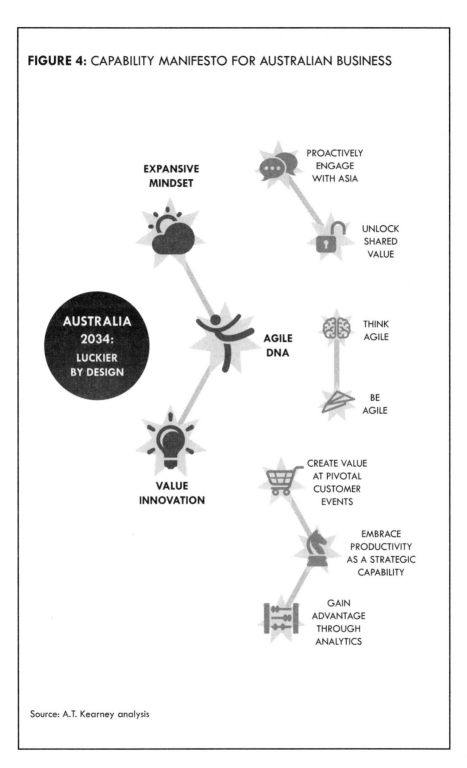

FIGURE 4: CAPABILITY MANIFESTO FOR AUSTRALIAN BUSINESS

PROACTIVELY ENGAGE WITH ASIA

EXPANSIVE MINDSET

UNLOCK SHARED VALUE

AUSTRALIA 2034: LUCKIER BY DESIGN

AGILE DNA

THINK AGILE

BE AGILE

VALUE INNOVATION

CREATE VALUE AT PIVOTAL CUSTOMER EVENTS

EMBRACE PRODUCTIVITY AS A STRATEGIC CAPABILITY

GAIN ADVANTAGE THROUGH ANALYTICS

Source: A.T. Kearney analysis

PROACTIVELY ENGAGE WITH ASIA

Asia represents a real opportunity for Australian business—not just in terms of trade but also in terms of talent, demography, and capital. But Asia has proved to be challenging. The region's market size, maturity, and price points make it an unfamiliar competitive environment with very different success factors and risk-return profiles, in need of more nuanced strategies.

Successfully and actively engaging with Asia demands a more thoughtful and considered approach than before. In contemplating the Asian opportunity, we suggest Australian businesses work through five principles:

- Recognize that there is no such thing as "Asia". Each market is complex, different, and demands a customised approach. We need to move away from discussing Asia as a monolithic market opportunity.
- Stress test the rationale why any given Australian business might succeed in Asia. Why Asia? Why us? and How? are three questions every board must ask. The answers are rarely clear and need thoughtful discovery.
- Reframe how we define success in these markets. Asia will pose a challenge in terms of risk and return horizons to Australian businesses with a quarter-on-quarter growth focus.
- Be thoughtful when formulating a go-to-market strategy for each country. Examine how to use local talent rather than expats whenever possible, and consider joining with non-traditional partners that have a keen understanding of these markets.
- Overcome internal roadblocks and address prevailing biases and misconceptions. The right governance architecture, injected with Asia-savvy talent, will be key.

UNLOCK SHARED VALUE

Business activity will continue to grow in volume and complexity—exponentially when measured in terms of GDP per capita. However, the social and environmental consequences of business activities, both positive and negative, are typically not considered or are addressed as an afterthought. As we look around at the wide range of social issues such as healthy eating, online privacy, responsible lending, and environmental stewardship, it becomes clear that politicians and regulators at times struggle to keep up. Furthermore, as industries mature, and products become commoditised, finding new sources of differentiation requires a broader perspective.

Companies have become more accountable, whether they like it or not—answering not only for what they achieve but for *how* they achieve it. In the long run there is a direct relationship between a company's success and the health of the related community.

Shared value, as professors Porter and Kramer define it, are "policies and operating practices that enhance the competitiveness of a company while simultaneously advancing the economic and social conditions in the communities in which it operates".[21] Doing so requires a new mindset that challenges the status quo, asks *why not*, and reformulates the very concept of how a business (and its stakeholders) define value. Strong, healthy societies are better markets.

Reviewing business strategies within a social and environmental context can point to a wide range of opportunities for innovation, new value creation, and improved efficiencies. The evidence that leading practitioners produce better shareholder returns is growing. Companies can create societal value—and hence economic value—by seeking to redefine productivity, reconceive products and markets, and develop local clusters. Waste is waste, and the negative side effects usually result in future problems. Indeed, the cost of avoidance is lower than subsequent remediation of pollution, excessive energy consumption, food waste, and the health impacts of many processed and packaged goods.

However, effective delivery can be challenging and will boil down to designing planning processes and an organisational structure that ensures that shared value creation is a priority across the business. This means fostering a culture that reinforces the commitment to shared value creation and bridging any capability gaps that may arise. To become sustainable, a new approach to measurement will also be needed. Shared value creation efforts will be short-lived if the full value—both to the company and its external stakeholders—cannot be measured in dollars and cents. Creating shared value is not something that can be handled by a corporate social responsibility task force.

CAPABILITY SET 2: INJECT AGILE DNA

An agile enterprise is one whose DNA embodies the ability and desire to change rapidly in response to opportunities and challenges. It has the capability and mindset to lead in dynamic conditions and implement change as a matter of routine in pursuit of a distinct purpose.

Joseph Schumpeter's observations on creative destruction are now more true than ever. Managing the transition from one generation to the next is challenging, and businesses of all types and sizes—not just small businesses and start-ups—fail to survive beyond 15 to 20 years. As disruption takes place, rapid responses are essential. The forces at work will both accelerate the demand for change and enable businesses to respond more quickly than ever before.

To become an agile enterprise requires agility in both thinking and behaviour. These are two separate but related capabilities, both of which are equally necessary.

THINK AGILE

A wide range of industries—computers, photography, and media, to name a few—have faced significant upheavals over the past two decades. More will follow, as changing global or local market conditions threaten firms' core assets or core activities, and as the value creation potential inherent in business operations is undermined and migrates to new players.

The business world is traditionally spoken of as comprising incumbents and challengers. We believe this view is outdated, because tomorrow's incumbents must behave like challengers. We also know that this is more easily said than done, because in many ways it is precisely a business's current formula for success that makes responding to disruptions so difficult.

Organisations are built and refined to efficiently provide goods and services within a well-defined market and competitive context. Executives develop mental models and biases derived from past experience to guide effective decision making. These biases must be recognised so that they do not become blinders. Efficient business practices and routines produce structural inertia that needs to be overcome to behave like a challenger. Also, responding to economic pressures and focusing plans on the more certain nearer term are engrained habits—habits that undermine the balance of exploiting current capabilities and exploring new capabilities and compromise longer-term investment and performance in favour of the short term.

Breaking out of this mould is possible. Adopting the rigour of viewing a business as a portfolio of capabilities will provide new insights. Distinguishing between assets and activities that will be valuable for future success and those that may be threatened will guide strategies to incubate next-generation value propositions, understand "salvageable" parts of the core that can be successfully transformed, and determine which business activities to exit. In parallel, however, governance models and incentive structures need to support both the use of existing capabilities and the development of new ones. Capital and ownership structures may also need to be revisited and more flexible structures for distinguishing stable cash flows from flexible growth investments explored.

BE AGILE

Success today by no means translates to success tomorrow in this fast-changing environment. Companies have honed their organisations to meet historic market conditions, structured to foster stability and control. Becoming an agile organisation is a concept that is widely recognised as critical for ongoing business success, yet is rarely seen. In our experience, three ingredients are part of the recipe:

- **Purposeful organisation**. A company needs to understand why it exists and what is the differentiating, distinct capability that allows it to successfully create value. It is this sense of purpose, communicated and demonstrated by inspiring leaders, that will engage the workplace and ensure an organisation remains flexible and creative about the "means to" while remaining focused and inspired by the "ends".

- **Operating model**. To be agile, a company's operating model needs to be clear and uncluttered. A lean and simple operating model requires effort to design, but once in place it leads to rapid decision-making processes backed by relevant incentives and measures, as well as to an optimal structure for demand-generating activities versus support services.

- **Diverse workforce**. We strongly believe in fostering a diverse workforce, not just in terms of social diversity but also in attitudinal and cognitive skills. Diversity brings new ideas, problem-solving approaches, and management styles, which are crucial to an agile organisation and a key weapon against organisational bias. Furthermore, offering different ways of working is a must to attract and retain highly talented people, particularly in this era of shifting demographics.

CAPABILITY SET 3: LEAD THROUGH INNOVATION

How companies create value is in flux. Value innovation is defined as a corporate capability to constantly understand, explore, tap into, and efficiently deliver new sources of value. To do so requires finding innovative ways to create customer value, embrace productivity as a strategic capability, and lead through analytics. Let's look at each of these in more detail:

CREATE VALUE AT PIVOTAL CUSTOMER EVENTS

Twenty years ago, business was ahead of customers. Today the tables have turned, with customers now racing ahead of business, increasingly demanding convenience and meaningful experiences, anytime and anywhere. Companies have responded by embracing customer centricity, focusing on "moments of truth" at customer contact points, simplifying their businesses, and streamlining processes.

Yet for many companies progress is slow and frustrating, and customer satisfaction is neutral at best. We believe a different approach is required to stay ahead of the tidal wave of commoditisation—an approach to first expand the company's thinking and then focus its execution of customer centricity. The approach revolves around defining and delivering truly differentiated experiences at "pivotal customer events"—these are the dozen or so windows into the relationship with the customer when value is really created both for the customer and the company. Pivotal customer events are more meaningful than moments of truth or touch points but less ambiguous than life stages. Together they represent a disproportionate amount of the value of customer centricity, but can be tackled at a fraction of the cost.

By discovering, designing, delivering, and embedding pivotal customer events, companies can find a more tangible focal point for everyone to rally around. Proper handling of these events must be articulated around emotions and customer effort, and not just around internal metrics such as touch times and turnaround times. The capability to engineer these events will be a hallmark of successful companies across sectors over the next 20 years. It is a capability that is both art and, increasingly, science.

EMBRACE PRODUCTIVITY AS A STRATEGIC CAPABILITY

Australia's productivity has been modestly increasing by an annual average rate of 0.3 per cent over the past 20 years, mostly thanks to improvements in technology, business practices, and regulation. However, over the past decade, productivity has actually decreased by 0.7 per cent annually. As the resource boom slows, Australia needs to reignite its productivity engine; should we fail to do so, the country will face the prospect of declining relative income and living standards. Australia's demographic trend will also add strength to the productivity case. Achieving productivity is essential to create the necessary headroom for innovation and investments that many, if not all, the capabilities outlined in this manifesto will demand.

Fortunately, the need to improve productivity is now well understood. It has been a topic of public debate for a number of years, with both public and private institutions suggesting recommendations. Productivity, however, can't just be shorthand for short-term cost cutting. To succeed in the next 20 years, Australian companies need to build true productivity over time.

We see productivity as a strategic capability, as something that is developed over three horizons: close the gap, maintain the lead, and change the game. Most companies are still only focusing on the first. To build productivity as a strategic capability is to establish the ability and the culture to sustainably boost productivity by focusing more on increasing the value being created than on reducing the cost base. The rather unsatisfactory alternative is to sawtooth between unproductiveness and productivity through sporadic cost-cutting programs.

Companies need to stop thinking of productivity as a "program" and start considering it a "capability". They need to inject productivity into how they do business: firstly, by focusing on productivity over multiple years on multiple fronts; secondly, by finding value beyond existing organisational boundaries; and finally, by innovating for productivity in both products and processes that keep a business running. The link between a firm's innovation activity and its productivity level and growth is empirically well established. Very few Australian companies, however, have reached this stage of capability maturity. We believe they will have to make progress up this productivity capability staircase over the next 20 years.

GAIN ADVANTAGE THROUGH ANALYTICS

In the coming two decades, analytics will become increasingly important. It is no longer going to be just about the data—"big" or otherwise. It is about building a pervasive analytics culture with a clear vision, strong capability, and C-suite support to leverage data-enabled insights that can fundamentally improve the competitive position of Australian companies.

What is the value of data? Unless data can be transformed into information, insight, and action, it is of little value to organisations and customers. The application of analytics will lead to efficiency and effectiveness improvements along the entire value chain, as well as enhance the customer experience and value propositions.

We see it as an important enabler of many of the capabilities we have outlined here for businesses to thrive over the next 20 years—especially in pivotal customer events, productivity, and agility, whose design and implementation require superior information and insight.

Leading through analytics requires investment not only in technology but also in human capital that can span organisational silos and external partnerships to unlock value embedded within ever growing reams of data. Central to achieving this is the integration of three distinct knowledge domains—business acumen, analytics acumen, and systems and IT acumen—to form "trilingual" analytics professionals, equally conversant in all three domains.

Creating this capability will be neither easy nor quick, but it will provide a basis of competitive advantage over the coming 20 years. Just as the IT staffer evolved into the IT manager and later into the CIO (chief information officer), we foresee the creation and advent of the chief data officer or chief analytics officer. This will require a rethink of the organisation at large—and of the people and culture in particular—to ensure that its actions support the growth of the analytics capability.

PREPARING FOR TOMORROW'S CHALLENGES

While it is impossible to predict the future, it is possible to prepare for it. By raising the bar of our expectations for Australian business, we can in turn raise our expectations for Australia and our fellow citizens for the next 20 years. In doing so, we pay homage to the past and to the efforts of those who shaped this period. Through the inspired leadership of current generations of business leaders, it is only fitting that our "Lucky Country" will be able to look back two decades from now and celebrate the profound role Australian business played in making Australia a country that is "Luckier by Design".

PART II: NURTURE AN EXPANSIVE MINDSET

CHAPTER 2

PROACTIVELY ENGAGE WITH ASIA

Much has been said about the opportunity Asia represents for Australia. The discussion often centres on China and focuses on the export of basic materials or the purchase of high-end properties in Australia by Asian investors. We have only begun to scratch the surface of the profound impact our proximity to the largest growth markets in the world might have on our business landscape.

Over the next 20 years, understanding and proactively navigating Asia will be an essential capability for Australian business. Asia will continue to develop rapidly, and Australian businesses could lose out on the opportunity to become serious regional players if they fail to engage. Some could even be driven out of their home market and cease to be viable concerns because of lack of scale.

The Australian government is beginning to realise the need to develop both our relationships and our capabilities domestically and in Asia, but much more remains to be done by government and the business community alike. Our focus is on Australian companies: we believe business leaders need to take a much broader view of why and how they can engage with Asia to create unprecedented value—and they need to be thinking about it now, before it's too late.

THREE LEVELS OF ASIAN-AUSTRALIAN INTEGRATION

The 21st century will be defined by Asia, with an impact that will be increasingly felt over the next 20 years. As touched on in our opening chapter, Asia's share of world output has already grown from 18 to 35 per cent over the past 60 years, and it will continue to be one of the world's fastest-growing regions.[22] Real GDP for emerging and developing Asia is expected to grow by more than 6.4 per cent per year at least until the next decade—a growth rate almost three times that of advanced economies and twice that of Australia.[23]

Our integration with Asia is already occurring on three levels—people, trade, and capital investment—all of which create new opportunities for Australian companies to increase their sphere of influence and capture new value.

With relatively smaller companies, shorter distances, and fewer time zones separating us from Asia compared with our global counterparts in other mature economies, Australian business is in a unique position to thrive in Asian markets if it sets its mind to it.

People. The face of Australia's immigrant population is shifting from Europe to Asia. Out of the five million non-native Australians living in our country today, two million were born in Asia. Compare this to 1981, when immigrants were primarily European and the Asian immigrant population only numbered 276,000. Immigration from Asia has grown 12 per cent yearly in the decade leading up to 2011, with China and India being the largest contributors.[24] And the movement between Asia and Australia is a two-way street: 40 per cent of Australian emigrants are now moving to Asia, a trend that will only intensify as economic opportunities increase in the region.[25] The growing Asia-fluent Australian workforce in both Australia and Asia could shift our ability to engage with Asia and help us transcend cultural and regional boundaries.

Trade. The centre of gravity of trade has shifted towards Asia over the past 20 years. The relative size of trade with the top three traditional trading partners in 1994 (United States, United Kingdom, and New Zealand) declined significantly, while the relative size of trade with China jumped from 4 to 23 per cent during the same period. Greater Asia now represents 62 per cent of Australia's trade in goods and services while Europe (14 per cent) and the Americas (11 per cent) trail far behind.[26] Until now, most trade with Asian countries has been resource focused. But Australia has a sophisticated skills and services sector, with capabilities that are in great demand in many developing Asian nations, which brings significant opportunities to export our ideas, innovation, and services. The financial services sector in particular, where Australian firms lead in wealth management, funds administration platforms, and digital innovations, should take note.

Capital. Asia attracts about one-third of all global foreign direct investment and remains a top potential destination for international investors over the next few years, with China ranking number two and India number seven in the A.T. Kearney FDI Confidence Index®.[27] The potential to attract foreign investment in a world challenged by cautious capital can be huge for Australian businesses that offer the right risk-reward profile.

The opportunity with Asia is significant, and our markets are integrating rapidly. Australian companies must now ask themselves if and how they must change in the next 20 years to succeed in what is now widely regarded as the Asian Century.

A TRACK RECORD OF CAUTIOUS ENGAGEMENT

Participation in Asia is nothing new for Australia. Our businesses have been in Asia since at least the 1960s, with our resource and construction services industries playing an active role in developing Asian infrastructure. But beyond these traditional players, Australian businesses at large have only begun seriously exploring Asia in the past decade.

Australian companies entering Asia typically begin with small investments and strong partnerships to bridge gaps in local knowledge. Over time, many have then tried to scale up—some more successfully than others. For example, in 1999, Insurance Australia Group (IAG) began its foray into the Asian market with a small investment in a Thai general insurance company. Seven years went by before its next move, when it invested in a Malaysian business in 2006. Since then, IAG has expanded its investments to India, China, and Vietnam through a portfolio of joint ventures, minority stakeholdings, and direct ownership models. Currently, the Asian businesses generate 7.1 per cent of IAG's premium income and are expected to be the driver of future growth.[28]

However, as Australia was testing the waters in Asia, competition from large global companies with significant scale advantages—among them HSBC, Prudential, and Aldi—began to intensify. In the early to mid-1990s, these companies began to grow market share aggressively, sometimes at a loss. Not only have large European and U.S. multinationals moved in to capture a portion of the growing Asian market, but Asian companies such as the International Commercial Bank of China, Samsung, and Huawei have also become multinationals with significant share in the Asian region.

While there are many cases of Australian companies operating successfully in Asia, few would argue that our business community at large has captured its full potential.

Australian companies run the risk of being too reluctant and complacent despite the opportunity on our doorstep. The growth of stronger, hungrier multinational companies willing to do more for market share has led sceptics to question how our companies will be able to compete in such a high-investment, fast-paced environment. We must answer this challenge emphatically and decisively in the next 20 years.

ENGAGING WITH ASIA: TIME FOR A MORE NUANCED APPROACH

To engage actively with Asia over the next 20 years, Australian business will need to recognise a few truths: there is no such thing as "Asia"; there is no easy strategy to create value in these markets; drag-and-drop business models will not work; navigating risk and return is not just a challenge but a core competence; partnerships are something to be crafted rather than endured; and governance must enable (rather than limit) an organisation's ability to think expansively.

In short, businesses will need to acknowledge that Asia requires—actually, it demands—a nuanced and sophisticated approach. Companies that embrace this reality could see their centre of gravity shift to Asia as it becomes their dominant region, making them true regional players and delivering significant growth and value in the longer term.

We describe the principles of this more modulated approach below (see figure 5):

UNDERSTAND THERE IS NO SUCH THING AS "ASIA"

Thinking of Asia as a monolith is a recipe for failure. Asia is made up of 27 countries and autonomous regions, with a population of almost 3.9 billion people. Even within one region or country, there are large economic and cultural differences (see figure 6).

FIGURE 5: ACTIVELY ENGAGING WITH ASIA

Principle	Current bias	Engaging Asia in the future

There is no such thing as "Asia" (Define your market)	• Treating Asia as one economy
	• Following the customer
		• Develop market-specific strategies, adapted to
		  – Diverse economies
		  – Different competitive sets

Be brutally clear on your value proposition	• Opportunistic value proposition "because Asia is large" • Entry using existing products or business models	• Be clear on product or capability offering and how you will win • Enter the market when the market is ready, or build demand early • Remember that Asia is not for everyone
Reframe your view of risk and return to the long term	• Short-term return horizons • Expectations of high margins, similar to the Australian market	• Think more broadly of returns: strategic (valuation multiple) as well as financial • Seek meaningful, long-term growth, casting aside existing business models and investment hurdles
Be creative with your "go-to-market" strategy	• Selective partnerships, typically with like-minded businesses	• Look up and down the value chain: be selective in what you want your partner to do • Partner with businesses within Australia to deliver compelling export "product packages"
Take a cosmopolitan perspective on risk management and governance	• Australian boards with strictly domestic expertise (and often strong aversion to risk) • Short-term ex-pat management teams	• Appoint board with Asian expertise and experience • Ensure management team has appropriate expertise and is incentivized for the long term; use the expanded "Australian" workforce in Asia

Source: A.T. Kearney

Because of China's size and growth, many Asia strategies tend to be China-centric. However, 16 Southeast Asian countries or autonomous regions have a population larger than Australia and will represent economic opportunities in their own right. Furthermore, China is a highly diverse market. The contrast between regions is large, and not every opportunity lies in the capital cities.

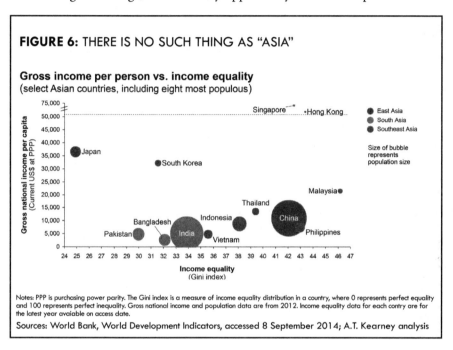

FIGURE 6: THERE IS NO SUCH THING AS "ASIA"

Gross income per person vs. income equality
(select Asian countries, including eight most populous)

Notes: PPP is purchasing power parity. The Gini index is a measure of income equality distribution in a country, where 0 represents perfect equality and 100 represents perfect inequality. Gross national income and population data are from 2012. Income equality data for each contry are for the latest year avaiable on access date.
Sources: World Bank, World Development Indicators, accessed 8 September 2014; A.T. Kearney analysis

The differences in economic maturity between (and indeed within) several Asian markets open up a broad range of opportunities. Less developed countries such as Myanmar, Laos, and Vietnam still require significant institution building and infrastructure, while more developed economies such as Hong Kong and South Korea will look for new waves of innovation and value creation. Over the next 20 years, the maturity of these fast-changing Asian economies will shift yet again: Malaysia, China, and Thailand could all become high-income developed countries, and lesser-known cities in China such as Chongqing and Guangzhou will rival Shanghai and Beijing in size.[29]

Another way to appreciate Asia's complexity is to look at it through the lens of a particular industry. Within a single industry, the size, maturity, concentration, and competitive intensity can vary substantially across Asia. The difference in industry consolidation in each country highlights opportunities and a view of timing for further industry concentration, which tends to progress along a set path with a pace driven primarily by economies of scale. For example, in the steel industry, China is still in the opening stages, providing opportunities for companies entering the market to define the industry and technology, set standards, and erect barriers to entry (see figure 7). India and Japan, on the other hand, are both heading towards the late stages of concentration: refining their business models, looking to gain volume, building confidence in their ability to absorb remaining smaller players, and exploring new market niches.

Beyond the economics, there are also religious, political, social, and legal differences between and within each country. Developing a strategy for Asia requires a much more considered and nuanced view of which markets are attractive, what stage their industries are at, and what products to bring to those markets. Australian companies should not lose sight of less popular countries and industries where the growth opportunity is still large compared to Australia and where they may have a relative advantage against local competitors.

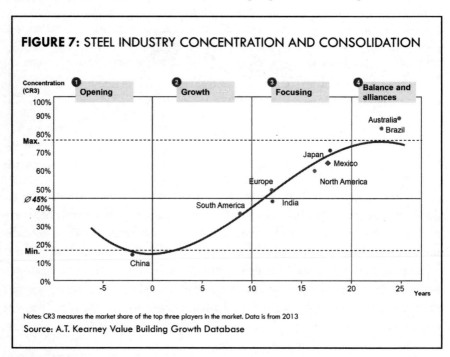

FIGURE 7: STEEL INDUSTRY CONCENTRATION AND CONSOLIDATION

Notes: CR3 measures the market share of the top three players in the market. Data is from 2013
Source: A.T. Kearney Value Building Growth Database

BE BRUTALLY CLEAR ON YOUR VALUE PROPOSITION

Drag-and-drop business models rarely work. With more experienced local players and ever more adaptable global entrants, the chances of an Australian company succeeding by simply transplanting its business model are close to zero.

For example, when Samsung entered the Indian market, it recognised that despite the company's advanced engineering capability, Samsung refrigerators were not suited to India's climate. The unstable electricity supply meant that fridges needed stabilisers and heavy insulation, and the strong aroma of Indian food meant they required more powerful filtering capacity. Samsung's ability to understand local consumers and tailor its products accordingly helped it capture a 22 per cent share of the Asian market by 2013.

The globalisation of Asia has brought about a more urban population with more worldly aspirations, and many companies have been successful with their uniquely foreign and forward-thinking capabilities and mindsets. The spare nature of the designs of H&M and IKEA from Sweden have seen both do very well in Asia: H&M had 205 stores in China alone at the end of 2013—up 53 per cent on the previous year, and IKEA's sales in Asia have doubled over the past decade. However, bringing in a competitive advantage will always require some level of local adaptation. For example, when IKEA entered China, it learned it had to tailor its store format to accommodate larger numbers of visitors; change its displays to show how the product would work in smaller living spaces; and significantly cut prices to be more competitive.

"Brand Australia" in itself is not yet a competitive advantage. In a September 2013 speech on access to global food markets, the CEO of the Australian Trade Commission (Austrade) acknowledged that much work remains to be done to strengthen and take advantage of the country's brand—and Asian retailers and distributors are clamouring for that to happen.[30]

Exceptions, however, do exist. For example, we are well-known for our health-conscious, relaxed, natural lifestyle. Aesop, an Australian cosmetics company famous for its plant-based products and minimalist approach, took its philosophy to Asia and found its niche in an unmet demand for more natural products, growing 30 per cent year on year between 2007 and 2013. Aesop has even declined to enter the Chinese market for fear of damaging its unique proposition—China requires all cosmetic manufacturers to test their products on animals prior to importing, a practice that Aesop opposes.[31]

The right customer proposition is often a matter of the right verb tense: *when* will the market be ready for something, rather than *what* is the market ready for now? The Asian consumer in the next 20 years will be very different from today—older, more affluent, more urban, and more cosmopolitan. Asia Pacific's share of the global middle class will be 66 per cent, compared with 28 per cent in 2009. In East Asia alone, the median age will increase by 10 years between 2010 and 2035, and 74 per cent of the population will live in urban areas compared to 54 per cent in 2010.[32] As incomes and the resulting middle class grow, the demand for more leisure products and more advanced products and services will increase. This creates an opportunity for Australian companies to become trendsetters in launching their unique propositions when the market is ready for them, or even creating demand for a trend that was not there.

The simplistic view that, because Asia is big, companies will find a home for their proposition, is naive. Asia is not for everyone. Companies that are unable to deliver a clear value proposition or to identify when and how they need to tailor their product may be better off not embarking on an Asian strategy but instead searching for opportunities in the domestic market.

REFRAME YOUR VIEW OF RISK AND RETURN TO THE LONG TERM

For many Australian companies, expanding into Asia is like leaving the safety of the local pool to go swimming in the ocean. They must be willing to invest and accept a different risk-return profile, but this does not necessarily mean more risk, less return. Returns can be both strategic and financial, with the former expressing themselves not in the profit and loss statement in the near term but rather in the valuation multiple, depending on the quality of the business and position being built. This view can be hard to navigate for a company focused on quarterly earnings.

Market leaders in Asia typically ride a J curve, supporting significant initial losses in order to establish a market-leading share in the longer term.

In 2006, SEEK, Australia's leading online job-search company, identified a long-term opportunity to capitalise on the rise of white-collar jobs in China. The company invested aggressively in Chinese job search firm Zhaopin with the goal of growing market share to hold leadership. The investment took five years to deliver a positive return (see figure 8). Today, Zhaopin holds the number two position in China in this field and is expected to become the world's largest online jobs market as more of China's citizens move to cities and use the Internet. SEEK's Asia expansion is continuing as it consolidates its number one ranking in several Southeast Asian countries. In early 2013, SEEK completed acquisition of the remainder of JobsDB and in 2014 announced its intent to acquire the remainder of the JobStreet business (subject to regulatory approvals).[33]

For the immediate future, the economics in Australia will tend to be far more attractive than in most of Asia because of low competition in many sectors of the economy. However, the maturity of the Australian market means lower growth prospects and tighter margins in the longer term, while Asia's promise will only continue to increase.

If existing ratios and targets are used as hurdles to assess investments in Asia, there will always be a temptation to focus on Australia alone. Last year, one of the main criticisms of the Australia and New Zealand Banking Group's (ANZ) Asian expansion strategy was that it could have earned better returns in the domestic market. However, as one analyst noted, "[ANZ Bank's] super-regional strategy can succeed, though returns are long-dated and shareholders need to be patient. … Returns will rise strongly if ANZ Bank executes successfully, though the upside comes with higher risks".[34]

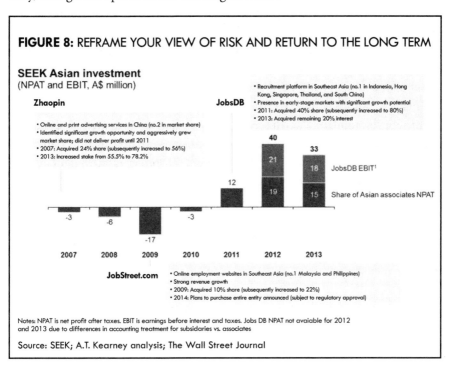

FIGURE 8: REFRAME YOUR VIEW OF RISK AND RETURN TO THE LONG TERM

SEEK Asian investment
(NPAT and EBIT, A$ million)

Zhaopin

JobsDB

• Recruitment platform in Southeast Asia (no.1 in Indonesia, Hong Kong, Singapore, Thailand, and South China)
• Presence in early-stage markets with significant growth potential
• 2011: Acquired 40% share (subsequently increased to 80%)
• 2013: Acquired remaining 20% interest

• Online and print advertising services in China (no.2 in market share)
• Identified significant growth opportunity and aggressively grew market share; did not deliver profit until 2011
• 2007: Acquired 24% share (subsequently increased to 56%)
• 2013: Increased stake from 55.5% to 78.2%

JobsDB EBIT[1]

Share of Asian associates NPAT

JobStreet.com

• Online employment websites in Southeast Asia (no.1 Malaysia and Philippines)
• Strong revenue growth
• 2009: Acquired 10% share (subsequently increased to 22%)
• 2014: Plans to purchase entire entity announced (subject to regulatory approval)

Notes: NPAT is net profit after taxes. EBIT is earnings before interest and taxes. Jobs DB NPAT not avaiable for 2012 and 2013 due to differences in accounting treatment for subsidaries vs. associates

Source: SEEK; A.T. Kearney analysis; The Wall Street Journal

The real risk lies not in Asia but at home: the risk that Australian companies and their shareholders will become too myopic, losing out in the long term because of their desire to maintain healthy profit margins and reduce risks in the short term. To be successful in Asia, Australian businesses need to move out of their comfort zone, take on a different risk profile, and redefine the metrics for success.

BE CREATIVE WITH YOUR GO-TO-MARKET STRATEGY

Australian companies entering Asian markets typically seek out like-minded (and safe) enterprises in the same industry with which to partner, either through a joint venture, a minority shareholding, or a distribution partnership. Few companies look up and down the value chain to determine where an Asian partner can provide the greatest value. Companies that do so, however, may find that non-traditional partnership models better serve their needs.

For example, foreign insurance companies with sophisticated products that were late to the Indian market were forced to look beyond the obvious financial and insurance players for partners with a large distribution footprint and advanced pricing capabilities. They found their counterparts in non-traditional partners such as telecoms players and retailers—for example, AXA with Bharti Airtel and Generali with the Future Group—which helped them create innovative propositions and grow in a crowded market. These are innovative go-to-market models.

Australian companies can also create partnerships within Australia to deliver export solutions. In the early 2000s, South Korea developed an e-government solution to place all civil services information on an online platform that is easily accessible for citizens. For instance, Koreans can now obtain birth certificates and social security information through self-service machines in government offices, reducing processing costs and time while increasing convenience. The government partnered with local software and telecoms providers to deliver a cross-industry solution that could be sold as a package to other governments. In 2011, exports of Korea's e-government solution reached US$200 million, having sold this product to countries such as Pakistan, Bangladesh, and the United Arab Emirates and picking up a United Nations administration prize along the way.[35]

According to MasterCard, Australia's readiness score for going cashless is 87 on a zero-to-100 scale, outperforming every other Asian market, including Japan, Korea, and Singapore.[36] Further innovation in this area and potential partnerships between Australian banks, telecoms, and software providers could create a compelling proposition for export to Asia. Once again, rethinking the business model and innovating the go-to-market approach would be keys to unlocking proactive engagement with Asia.

TAKE A COSMOPOLITAN PERSPECTIVE ON RISK MANAGEMENT AND GOVERNANCE

Boards and governance can either facilitate or constrain engagement with Asia. Boards and senior management teams with the right mix of experience and backgrounds can ensure that risk management and governance support successful outcomes.

More Australian companies are appointing directors with significant Asian experience. IAG recently named the former finance director in Singapore to its board, and Treasury Wine Estates appointed the former president and CEO of Walmart China as a director in 2012.

While risks need to be monitored at corporate levels, execution still has to happen locally, so companies must be structured to combine high-level supervision with deep local expertise and autonomy. Three-year expatriate assignments can create a short-term view of growth, but they also limit management's ability to truly understand local markets, cultures, and ways of doing business. Imagine how difficult such a task is in India, where there are 122 official languages; or in Korea, which has nine levels of respect language to master.

Successful companies have recognised this. Since 1990, Samsung has sent promising young employees abroad for one year. Many firms assign employees to foreign affiliates, but what's unique about Samsung is what employees aren't expected to do. "They don't work," says Tae Gyun Shin, president of Samsung's Human Resources Center. "They are given three missions: learn the local language, learn the local culture, and become an expert in their specialty". Since the program began 23 years ago, more than 5,000 employees have participated. In fact, Shin himself took part in the program in 1995.[37]

Furthermore, Samsung's global mobility program is a "reverse placement" plan that provides the opportunity for employees outside of Korea to work at the company's headquarters or other international subsidiaries. This program promotes globalisation of resources and gives employees an opportunity to become worldwide leaders.

Closer to home, SEEK's Asian investment philosophy states it will only get involved in advising management teams on corporate and business strategy. At Zhaopin, SEEK has put in place a Chinese-born, U.S.-educated management team with domestic and international experience. The trend to leverage local or Australian talent with a deep understanding of Asian markets is a positive one that, in time, is likely to replace the "exported expatriate" model. This trend is particularly timely as the pool of human capital and talent from immigrants in Australia and the expanded emigrant Australian workforce in Asia provides an opportunity to tap into the management expertise of many Australians who are immersed in Asian culture, and vice versa. Australian companies that are serious about developing long-term positions overseas need to ensure that the right structures and people are in place.

STRESS TESTING WHERE YOU ARE TO DETERMINE WHERE YOU NEED TO GO

The next 20 years represent an unprecedented opportunity for Australia to grow with our Asian neighbours. The expansion of foreign and Asian multinationals in the region has already led many to question how we can compete in today's fast-paced environment. The reality is that there are no easy plays. Businesses must think carefully about where, what, and how they compete to capture value as Asian markets develop over the next 20 years. A new level of maturity must be reached in how we, as a business community, think about, discuss, and tackle the Asian challenge.

Testing your current Asia strategy against the five principles outlined above is a useful exercise for probing the maturity of any Asian strategy. Questions that arise may range from fundamental ones such as "Are Asian markets in or out of your strategy for the right reasons?" to detailed ones such as "What metrics are you using to define your success in Asia. Are these the right ones? Are you setting yourself up for success or failure in Asia with these metrics?"

If these questions are uncomfortable and difficult to answer, you are probably on the right track in honing your organisation's capability for proactive engagement with Asia.

CHAPTER 3

UNLOCK SHARED VALUE

Markets are evolving and becoming more complex. Business activity continues to grow—exponentially when measured in terms of GDP per capita. However, the social and environmental consequences of business activities, both positive and negative, are typically either not considered or are an afterthought. As we look around at the wide range of social issues from healthy eating and online privacy to responsible lending and environmental stewardship, it is clear that politicians and regulators often struggle to keep up.

The way the world communicates is also changing. Social media is giving a louder and clearer voice to a broad range of stakeholders that are directly or indirectly impacted. Hiding behind a veil of secrecy and opacity is no longer an option for companies or for governments. Information travels at lightning speed, and social media makes everyone a potential journalist.

Companies have become more accountable, whether they like it or not—answering not only for what they achieve but for how they achieve it. The implications of heightened accountability extend beyond internal operations to affect suppliers, customers, and consumers alike. All become cogs in a wheel that serves—or disserves—the community.

Furthermore, as markets grow and mature, competition intensifies and business activity becomes more commoditised. Given that a business and its role in society are clearly interlinked, it stands to reason that taking a broader view of the ecosystem should provide a wider range of differentiation opportunities.

What exactly does this mean? It means businesses that solely focus on increasing next quarter's earnings will very likely be penalised in the medium to long term. In a way, it's an evolution of the maxim that "the customer is always right" into "the community is always right". In other words, pursuing a broader business purpose offers greater potential for positive differentiation and long-term damage to stakeholders in the company's extended ecosystem is likely to undermine the company's very sustainability. Michael Porter and Mark Kramer call this concept shared value creation (SVC).[38]

In this chapter, we will briefly review the concept and rationale, but our primary focus will be on how businesses are applying SVC, why it is good business, the typical challenges, and how success should be measured. Australian companies would do well to take note, as SVC can offer a new lens for seeing value creation and will be key to their success over the next two decades.

WHAT IS SHARED VALUE CREATION?

The core idea of shared value creation and related concepts, such as purpose-driven business, managing for stakeholder value, and conscious capitalism, is that there is a direct relationship between a company's success and the health of the related stakeholder communities, including customers, suppliers, employees, shareholders, and other community members. Porter and Kramer define the concept as "policies and operating practices that enhance the competitiveness of a company while simultaneously advancing the economic and social conditions in the communities in which it operates. Shared value creation focuses on identifying and expanding the connections between societal and economic progress".[39] The corollary of this concept is that a company that manages the conditions of the community well will be rewarded with improved competitiveness and success.

SVC can supersede corporate social responsibility (CSR) in guiding a company's investment in its community. CSR programs are concerned mostly with reputation and have a limited connection to the business, making them hard to justify and maintain over the long run. In a study A.T. Kearney conducted with the Committee for Melbourne for the United Nations Global Compact Principles for Social Investing Secretariat, we found that for 55 lead companies, 85 per cent of social investments are essentially philanthropic. SVC, in contrast, is integral to a company's profitability and competitive position. It leverages the company's unique resources and expertise to generate economic value by creating social value.

The concept gained currency in the turbulent period of the late 2000s, when confidence in business plummeted and awareness of the potentially negative social impact of certain business practices was exacerbated. The 2008 financial crisis, and in particular predatory lending practices and the subprime mortgage scandal in the United States, was a seminal moment that highlighted the risks some very prominent businesses were prepared to take at the expense of the broader community in their quest to maximise profits—with a government backstop in case things went terribly wrong, as indeed they did.

Thus, two forces are leading the drive for SVC: the community and shareholders.

PULL FROM THE COMMUNITY

Citizens are shifting their faith from government to business to resolve societal issues. According to the 2014 Edelman Trust Barometer, trust in business is 16 points higher than in government, and the gap continues to widen. Not only do communities now trust business more than government, but "84 per cent of respondents believe that business can pursue its self-interest while doing good work for society".[40] As people lose faith in the political system, they are pinning their hopes on the power of companies to develop efficient solutions and act more decisively to create change.

But while people are placing greater trust in businesses, they are also watching them closely. Social media make it easy for community interest groups and non-governmental organisations to spread their message far and wide, and antisocial practices can quickly harm a company's reputation—as the venerable Australian sporting goods manufacturer Sherrin discovered when it was found to be using underage, underpaid labour to hand-stitch footballs for an Australian sports league.

Organisations, then, must pay greater heed to their reputations. While trust is a good barometer of future business success, missteps in areas such as climate change, deforestation, and labour practices all have the potential to derail the positive momentum.

PUSH FROM SHAREHOLDERS

Companies have traditionally assumed that governments tax all externalities generated by their business activities. Moreover, they have taken for granted that suppliers, consumers, and other stakeholders are fully aware of those externalities and are therefore equipped to make well-informed trade-off decisions. As a result, executives have drawn the obvious conclusion that they should source all inputs from the supplier offering the best value and sell their goods at the highest price the market will bear. Not surprisingly, this logic has led businesses to largely exclude the social and environmental impact of their decisions.

There's a problem with this, though. The underlying assumption is false. This focus on the direct profit equation typically overlooks the fact that businesses operate in an interdependent ecosystem with a more complex value equation. Value is maximised when all stakeholders benefit, in the short and long term. Governments are unable to tax many externalities for a variety of political, economic, and scientific reasons. Furthermore, certain more indirect externalities only become apparent months or years after a transaction is concluded, meaning stakeholders are often unaware of the trade-offs they are making.

Many of the externalities that companies create can come back to haunt them. That's why shareholders are beginning to demand that executives price them into their strategic decision-making processes. In some cases, businesses may find that by working with the community, they are able to increase the value for everyone. Even if most of the benefits accrue to other stakeholders in the value chain, the additional value created increases the profit pool for everyone. And there's another benefit: by strengthening the bonds with employees, customers, and suppliers, stickiness increases and thereby improves the company's long-term viability.

SVC IN ACTION

Many companies have already begun to embrace SVC. Local supermarkets are working with charities to put surplus food to good use and with environmental groups to reduce the impact of plastic bags. Large global food companies are working with farmers to improve local crop prices and yields and to build more efficient logistical networks. In developing countries, some companies are working with local partners to tailor their goods and services to consumers' actual needs.

Importantly, the market is showing faith in companies that are taking the lead in social and sustainability measures, as social investment indexes outperform the market as a whole. For example, a benchmark report on responsible investment in Australia and New Zealand found that responsible investment funds are delivering better returns than both the benchmark and the average of all mainstream funds over three, five, and 10 years.[41] As a result, shareholders are starting to ask corporate management teams exactly what steps they are taking to unlock shared value. Some compelling answers exist within our shores.

COLES SUPERMARKETS AND RED GROUP

Coles was just one of many major retailers to look across its value chain and discover the economic and environmental consequences of free disposable plastic grocery bags. As a result, the grocer began to sell reusable bags—to reduce waste, generate a new revenue stream, and lower costs.

At the same time, a small recycling company called RED Group began looking at how to address the problem of plastic shopping bags and other soft plastics that ordinary household waste recycling services will not accept. RED Group identified a specialised company that could process soft plastics and set up a pilot collection system at schools—allowing them to gather raw material while also educating students about the importance of recycling. Later, RED Group partnered with Coles to install collection points at nearly 150 stores, providing 70 per cent of Australians with convenient access to soft plastics recycling bins. The program collects as many as 250,000 bags per week and recycles them into outdoor furniture that is donated to primary schools across the country.[42]

Besides addressing a significant environmental concern, the program generates shared value for a wide range of stakeholders. It delivers social value to the community through increased environmental awareness and furniture donations to schools, financial value to RED Group through a commercially viable business model, and tangible and intangible value to Coles through reduced costs and increased goodwill.

WESTPAC DAVIDSON INSTITUTE

In 2011, Australian financial services provider Westpac created the Davidson Institute to provide financial education to consumers, small businesses, and not-for-profit organisations. The institute offers short courses and free seminars on financial and business planning topics including budgeting, cash flow management, investing, and managing debt. Westpac had begun offering financial education to small business owners back in 2003 but later found that many other customer segments shared the need for better financial management.

The Davidson Institute creates value for the community because improved financial literacy helps people make sounder financial decisions, making it more likely they will achieve their financial and personal goals. Thus, the productivity and wealth of the entire community is enhanced.

Westpac, too, derives value from the program. The program is designed to reduce the risk of loan default by customers who undertake the courses. In addition, the courses provide an opportunity for Westpac to present its own financial solutions while also potentially creating positive relationships for the future. The institute also provides training to Westpac staff, who can apply the knowledge to manage their own finances better and to serve the bank's customers more effectively.

RIO TINTO

For many years, large mining companies in the northwest of Western Australia mostly relied on fly-in, fly-out workers to develop and operate their mines. Although these outside workers were needed to quickly ramp up activity in the beginning, this staffing model caused the economic benefits of the mining boom to largely flow back to Perth and other metropolitan centres, leaving little behind in the local communities.

With time, the mining companies have begun to re-evaluate their approach. They realised that over the longer term, this formula is unsustainable as local communities are unable to invest in the infrastructure and provide the services needed for efficient mining operations. Therefore, companies have made a concerted effort to increase local employment as well as the share of goods and services purchased in nearby communities.

Rio Tinto, for example, has established a community program near its operations. In the Pilbara region, it has invested in early literacy and numeracy programs, as well as in post-secondary education and training, mental and family health initiatives, cultural development projects, and environmental and regional sustainability development programs. At its Argyle diamond mine in the Kimberly region, Rio Tinto has worked with one of its largest service providers, Spotless, to develop and train local workers.

Although these initiatives require significant upfront investment, they ensure the health of the local communities on which these companies rely. And in the long term, they lead to lower labour and transport costs.

RAISING OUR GAME

Despite instances of companies moving in the right direction, SVC has not yet been widely adopted in Australia. The answer, we believe, has much to do with today's cost-conscious environment, where businesses focus on improving operational efficiency to maintain short-term returns, while longer-term investments compete intensively for funding.

And the truth is there are few glowing examples of local businesses that have built their profitability by creating value for the entire community—usually because of pitfalls such as an insufficiently ambitious SVC strategy, lack of integration of the SVC delivery resources in the company's key operations and business lines, or loosely defined value expectations.

We propose three ways to overcome these pitfalls (see figure 9).

ADOPT A TRANSFORMATIONAL SVC STRATEGY

The starting point for formalising an SVC strategy is the company's core purpose—its reason for being—often captured in its mission, vision, and value statements. The more clearly this purpose is articulated, particularly with respect to how the business is trying to make a difference in the world, the better it can act as a guide for formulating an SVC strategy.

A transformational SVC strategy then scopes opportunities across the value chain. According to Porter and Kramer, companies can create societal value—and hence economic value—in three ways (see figure 10).[43]

Redefine productivity across the value chain. Opportunities to elimi-

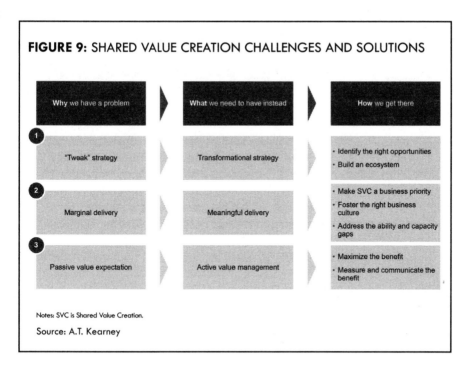

FIGURE 9: SHARED VALUE CREATION CHALLENGES AND SOLUTIONS

nate waste or increase efficiency can exist anywhere in the system. Companies that scour the value chain looking, for instance, at resource inputs, energy consumption, logistics and distribution networks, and workforce configurations are certain to find opportunities to unlock shared value. It is important to look not just at the company's own assets and operations, but also to partner with other stakeholders to discover areas of mutual benefit.

Nestlé's work with the South Australian Research Development Institute's (SARDI) national oat breeding program and with local producers exemplifies this approach. The food multinational is working with farmers within 100 kilometres of its largest manufacturing plants to help them increase crop productivity and yield, while collaborating with SARDI to develop new drought- and pest-resistant varieties of oats. In addition to the obvious benefits to Australian producers, Nestlé will reap savings in the longer term by reducing the need to import oats from Canada.

Reconceive products and markets. Companies can look across their products and services portfolio for opportunities to redesign or reposition them to take on social or environmental issues or to generate additional profits by addressing untapped customer segments—for example, at the bottom of the pyramid. Doing so often requires significant innovation capabilities to change

FIGURE 10: ADOPT A TRANSFORMATIONAL SVC STRATEGY

Opportunity identification	Key questions to consider
Redefine productivity across the value chain	• Where is the waste in our value chain (for example, input resources, energy use, logistics, distribution)? Which stakeholders can potentially reduce the waste?
	• Where is long-term benefit being crowded out by compromised short-term investment (for example, fly-in, fly-out workforce)?
Reconceive products and markets	• Which of our products and services fulfil a basic need? Which markets cannot yet access these products or services?
	• What are the major social or environmental issues where we operate? Which of our products and services, if tailored, can address these issues?
Develop local clusters	• What are the current market gaps or failures among the industries where we operate? What assets would we need to develop to address them?
	• Which local communities do we operate in and what are their major social needs?

Notes: SVC is Shared Value Creation.

Sources: Michael E. Porter and Mark R. Kramer. "Creating Shared Value", Harbard Business Review 89, no. 1/2 (2011): 62-77; A.T. Kearney

production and distribution costs, scope, quality and features of offers, and consumer experience. Sometimes, governments and NGOs can be convinced to provide monetary or other support to reward the positive externalities created. Although products and services in this space may overlap with those of non-profit organisations, for-profit companies are often better equipped to deliver them.

For example, Vodafone and SafariCom launched the well-known M-Pesa product, which enables customers in Tanzania and Kenya to deposit, withdraw, and transfer money on their mobile phones using prepaid accounts. By reconceiving mobile phone service, the carriers created significant value for local communities, providing accessible basic financial services to large swathes of socially disadvantaged people, even in remote villages.

Develop local clusters. Many of the opportunities discussed above result from innovation and a new way of thinking about products and services across the business—often from partnering with other organisations to bring this innovation to the table. Innovation is typically most successful when strong partnerships are developed in a cluster environment—that is, when a variety of corporate, research, and educational institutions team up within a geographic, or even a virtual, space.

Clusters can, for example, help participants address gaps in the enabling environment such as a lack of skilled workers, a paucity of research or testing facilities, insufficient infrastructure, and inexperience in dealing with complex regulatory issues. While some clusters emerge naturally, others are catalysed by one or two organisations, typically working in partnership with educational institutions.

INTEGRATE SVC DELIVERY RESOURCES INTO KEY OPERATIONS AND BUSINESS LINES

While developing a transformational SVC strategy is a prerequisite to success, the ability to deliver on that strategy is paramount. Effective delivery boils down to designing an organisational structure that ensures that SVC is a priority across the business—fostering a culture that reinforces the commitment to SVC and bridging any capability gaps that may arise.

Structure and align the organisation to make SVC a business priority. Few companies have invested heavily in SVC initiatives. Those that have are typically an outgrowth of CSR, figuratively sitting off to one side of the business under a person who is not accountable for the company's revenue or profitability, and does not stand to benefit from the impact of SVC.

Ideally, the people responsible for the various stages of the SVC life cycle should be those who stand to receive the most benefits (see figure 11). Thus, accountability best resides with key line and business managers, whose performance targets need to incorporate the results of SVC initiatives.

Foster a reinforcing business culture. Companies can create the right business culture for SVC success by following four guidelines:

- **Link SVC explicitly to the mission statement.** Clearly articulate the mission that the company wishes to fulfil and the value (in monetary terms) SVC will create. For example, if health is part of the overall mission, SVC could focus on reduced cost of care or lower loss of productive days because of improved health. A tight link increases the likelihood that employees will hold themselves accountable for following through.
- **Go bottom up, tapping into staff energy.** When staff are inspired by, and aligned with, a company's broader purpose and feel that they are shaping a process and are being listened to, they are more inclined to commit to ongoing success. Nurture those who take an interest in SVC, as they are the most likely to support, foster, and grow the ideas.
- **See stakeholder consensus as an essential factor for success.** Both in-

FIGURE 11: SVC LIFE CYCLE RESPONSIBILITY

SVC life cycle component	Responsible role
Identify opportunities	Head of strategy, with support from functions
Prioritize opportunities	CEO, with support from functions
Implement	Incubator team and business unit executive manager
Monitor	Business unit executive manager
Embed and scale	Business unit executive manager

Notes: SVC is Shared Value Creation.

Source: A.T. Kearney

ternal and external stakeholders' support is needed for success, so consider all views and seek interdependent value creation and win-wins among employees, suppliers, customers, management, and the community. Failing to achieve external consensus is a recipe for failure and can leave a company with less goodwill than it had before it began.

- **See SVC as an opportunity to hone innovation and agility.** SVC requires reaching beyond natural instincts to search for, identify, and try out new ideas continually—and be prepared to shelve those that aren't gaining traction. This environment must be fostered, encouraged, and consistently reinforced. In chapter five, we discuss the need to develop agile organisations that are purposeful, fit, and diverse. These characteristics are essential to creating the mindset and capabilities to pursue SVC successfully.

- **Bridge any capability gaps that arise.** Many companies do not have the capability or capacity to tackle every aspect of the SVC initiatives they identify. In particular, mature businesses are geared to maximise profit from well-established business lines and therefore may lack the portfolio management capabilities to take on a range of innovative opportunities that change the way the business operates. We have a few words of advice:

  - **Adopt a disruptor's mindset.** Chapter four provides a discussion of the skills and capabilities needed to adopt a disruptor's mindset. Suffice it to say that SVC requires a deep understanding of a company's core assets and activities—and a willingness to challenge them head-on.

  - **Reconfigure for long-term optimisation.** SVC initiatives require business structures that are adapted to a long-term mindset. The capital structure, for example, needs to reflect that the company is looking for returns further down the horizon, and management incentives must also recognise that reality. In addition, key parts of the business (such as the incubator team) need to be given a long-term mandate to invest in ideas and businesses and be confident that they have the backing to manage the portfolio of opportunities.

- **Reimagine relations with external stakeholders.** For many businesses, relationships with the broader community are purely transactional: suppliers provide goods to a particular specification, at a specific location, for a price, as determined by a contract. An SVC approach requires a different sort of engagement, based on openness and trust, a willingness to share and collaborate, and an egalitarian approach—regardless of each party's relative strength. In some ways, it's like a new job: things are likely to be strange and unfamiliar at the outset as the parties grow accustomed to one another.

DEFINE AND MEASURE VALUE EXPLICITLY

SVC efforts will be in vain if the company does not know the value it expects to achieve and whether it is, in fact, achieving it. Although the expected qualitative benefits of SVC initiatives are often clearly defined, the real challenge is to evaluate their economic benefit in dollars and cents, both to the company and to its external stakeholders. Furthermore, the value needs to be measured in such a way that business units can monitor the results and take corrective action if they fall short of the target.

Figure 12 sets out three CSR approaches that many businesses are now applying more broadly to SVC. While each approach has its uses, none is perfect, and they continue to evolve to attempt to capture the full value an SVC initiative creates for a business and its stakeholders. Other alternatives include the social return on investment methodology or classic economic modelling techniques. These alternatives have limitations too, but their ability to estimate SVC benefits in economic terms is important to enable companies to prioritise their investments, monitor and manage execution, and communicate results.

Whatever the methodology, we have identified four levels of maturity in measuring shared value (see figure 13).

- Companies with a **qualitative view** detail the tangible, qualitative benefits of SVC initiatives but do not yet measure the economic ones. This is common in many organisations with CSR, where initiatives are developed and implemented as an add-on to the core business, with the main objective of generating positive perceptions.

FIGURE 12: CSR MEASURES BEING EXTENDED TO SVC STRATEGY

Approach	Description	Pros	Cons
Environmental, social and corporate governance (ESG)	• Environmental, social, and governance issues or factors are incorporated into investment analysis	• Used heavily for a number of years • Supported by a set of responsible investing principles developed by the UN	• ESG factors are not consistent across industries • Debate continues about the inclusion of intangible factors relating to the sustainability and ethical impact of investments
Triple bottom line	• Alongside the traditional bottom line of profit, the triple bottom line adds two more "bottom lines": social and environmental (ecological) concerns	• Captures social and environmental benefits (and costs) as well as traditional financial performance measures	• Measurement is not standardised across people, planet, and profit, so the three "bottom lines" cannot be added together
Program logic	• Aims to link investments with results based on a chain of logic, defining what a project will do and how it will do it	• Qualitative outcomes are clearly defined • Helps make assumptions explicit • Is useful as an effective planning tool	• Does not provide a measure of outcomes or a methodology for assigning economic value • Cannot be standardised across initiatives or companies

Notes: CSR is Corporate Social Responsibility, SVC is Shared Value Creation.

Source: A.T. Kearney

- Firms taking an **initiative view** quantify stakeholder impact from individual SVC initiatives in dollar terms. For example, a company with three different initiatives may measure the economic benefits of each one in order to track progress and manage success, but the methodology is inconsistent across initiatives, and results are not consolidated.
- The **portfolio view** quantifies initiatives using a standardised methodology that enables the aggregation of value and a single dollar view of all returns. Such a methodology is developed centrally and then rolled out.
- In a **holistic view**, the value the company creates across all of its activities for all of its stakeholders is quantified and communicated, including the share of value captured by each of them. This level of maturity goes a step further than the portfolio view, in that it attempts to measure the shared value created not just by SVC initiatives but also by normal, ongoing business activities.

The vast majority of companies that have embraced SVC still take a qualitative or, at best, an initiative view. Yet a handful of companies have moved further up the ladder. One example is Puma, which uses an environmental profit and loss statement in which a monetary value is assigned to all of the company's impacts on the environment, including water use, greenhouse gas emissions, land use, and waste generation—thus making it easier to monitor the outcomes of specific initiatives. In another example, Shell Australia has begun to use social

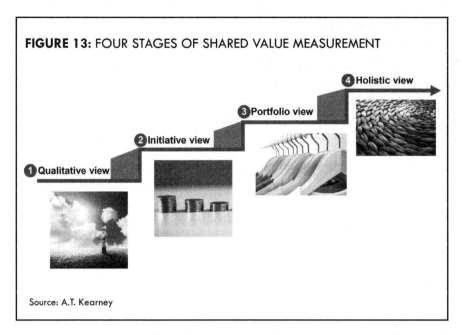

FIGURE 13: FOUR STAGES OF SHARED VALUE MEASUREMENT

❶ Qualitative view

❷ Initiative view

❸ Portfolio view

❹ Holistic view

Source: A.T. Kearney

return on investment methodologies to value the economic impact of its social investment portfolio and prioritise them based on the returns generated.

An interesting case study of how these three themes—a transformation strategy, integrated delivery, and explicit value measurement—are being put into action is social enterprises (see sidebar: Social Enterprises: A Different Perspective on Value Creation).

THE NEXT WAVE OF GROWTH

SVC is not just the latest fad. Rather, it will become essential for tomorrow's businesses, not only to improve their corporate reputations but also to think more expansively about value within and beyond their organisations.

This shift is not an easy one to make. Businesses will need the visionary leadership to drive and build belief across the organisation, along with the strategy, delivery, and value-management to make SVC work and last.

Those that are able to muster the vision and leadership early on and take the lead in reshaping the way they think about communities will see the benefits evolve over time. In 20 years, they will be operating in a world where they are well-respected and trusted by the local community—and where their organisation is intertwined and working productively with stakeholders to identify, create, and deliver sustainable value, continually, across the value chain.

SOCIAL ENTERPRISES:
A DIFFERENT PERSPECTIVE ON VALUE CREATION

One type of organisation that illustrates the themes of a transformation strategy, integrated delivery resources, and explicit value management—albeit on a smaller scale—is the social enterprise. The primary purpose of social enterprises is to create a public or community benefit, using trading to generate revenue and fulfil their objective. They focus on creating value for the community, not just for shareholders.

Social enterprise in Australia is growing rapidly, with revenue now estimated to account for nearly 3 per cent of GDP.[44] This confirms there is strong consumer demand for businesses that deliver a benefit to society.

Social enterprises are a good illustration of the key themes we've just outlined:

- They have defined their business strategy to serve a different purpose from conventional businesses in their categories, which they have clearly articulated and defined. This has usually involved either redefining the value chain, as SecondBite has done by delivering excess goods from the food production value chain to people in need; or by reconceiving products and markets—as in the case of LeapFrog, a micro insurance player looking to reduce the cost of risk in emerging markets.

- Their business models and operations are designed to deliver value to the community. By starting with a clear social purpose, they are able to design their operations specifically to achieve their objective.

- They focus on measuring the social benefit they have created rather than the financial results they have achieved. For example, Thankyou Water measures the number of people in developing countries that are aided by its programs, and reports the impact via its website almost in real time, while STREAT reports the number of hours of training it provides to homeless youth. Clearly defined measures of social benefit allow these companies to monitor their performance against their defined purpose and provide feedback to the wider community on the benefits they are creating.

Undoubtedly, it is much more challenging for traditional businesses to embrace SVC than for social enterprises to do so, in that conventional companies need to create value for multiple stakeholders across the entire value chain, whereas social enterprises are primarily focused on the community. Social enterprises, however, provide a good example of how to think about business from a different perspective. The question for traditional corporations is how to incorporate some of the DNA of a social enterprise into their own organisation to create enhanced value for the community and society.

PART III:
INJECT
AGILE DNA

CHAPTER 4

THINK AGILE

ELUDING THE CROSSHAIRS OF DISRUPTION

Businesses around the world are under growing pressure from a wide range of trends, such as demographic changes, the rebalancing of global production and consumption patterns, technological discoveries and innovations, resource scarcity, dislocation, and price volatility, plus various geopolitical forces.

The impact these trends will have on Australian businesses, including the severity and speed with which they affect markets and companies, will differ by industry. Rather than analysing these trends and the underlying drivers in great detail, our focus here is to consider the broader question of industry change and how companies can develop winning strategies for surviving change.

The track record for companies' survival is rather alarming. In Australia, of the top 100 companies in the ASX 100 in 1994, only 29 were still part of the Index in 2013. Of the 71 companies that exited the top 100, 51 were either acquired or merged with other businesses. The rest were delisted, dropped in the rankings, or went bankrupt.[45] The survival rate in other countries is not much better.[46]

Maintaining superior performance in the face of changing industry dynamics is difficult, as companies tend to get caught in the crosshairs between market share and profitability (see figure 14). What can businesses do to move from their current business model to one that will let them thrive tomorrow? How can they outwit the conditions that put them in the crosshairs of disruption? We believe the answer lies in confronting the challenge and plotting their own disruption.

This chapter defines what we mean by disruption, examines why it is so challenging to address, and proposes an approach for businesses to plot their own disruption and thereby avoid getting caught in the crosshairs.

DEFINING DISRUPTION

Industry change and disruption have been a research topic at business schools for a while now. A wide range of industries have faced significant upheaval during

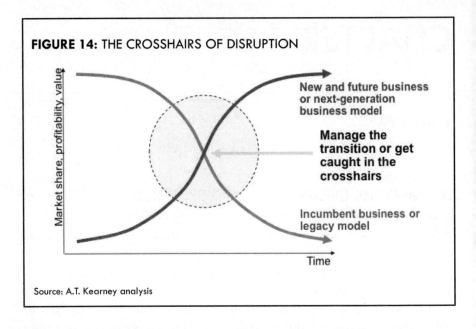

FIGURE 14: THE CROSSHAIRS OF DISRUPTION

New and future business or next-generation business model

Manage the transition or get caught in the crosshairs

Incumbent business or legacy model

Market share, profitability, value

Time

Source: A.T. Kearney analysis

the past two decades. For example, in the computer industry, market presence shifted from Compaq to Dell and eventually to Apple, while mainframes were replaced by minicomputers, which were replaced by desktop computers. Today, the desktop computer's successor, laptops, are being replaced by tablets and smartphones.

In photography, as the analogue print was replaced by digital photography, we witnessed the fall of Polaroid, Kodak, and Canon and the rising technology of mobile phone cameras, with Apple and Samsung now leading the way.

In media, online news threatens newspapers, and online content is replacing video stores. News organisations face the dilemma of reallocating resources to attract new readers and viewers while still trying to hold on to their existing—and usually ageing—print or broadcast audiences.

University of Toronto Professor Anita M. McGahan says industries evolve along four trajectories: radical, creative, intermediating, and progressive.[47] We have borrowed this definition to characterise industry disruption as occurring when a firm's core assets or core activities—or both—are threatened by changing global or local market conditions. McGahan defines core assets as the firm's durable resources, including production equipment and intangibles such as specialised knowledge, patents, and brand that make the firm more efficient at performing core activities. Core activities are recurring actions performed to conduct business and attract and retain suppliers and buyers.

Radical change—when a firm's assets and activities are threatened—is often driven by technology, whereby the whole industry is transformed. Travel agencies are a good example. Intermediating change is when relationships are fragile and a firm's activities, but not its assets, are threatened; think investment brokerages. Creative change is when the industry constantly redevelops assets and resources but core activities survive, as has happened in the motion picture industry. Progressive change is characterised by more incremental innovation, with firms leveraging their assets and core activities for ongoing value creation.

McGahan observed that radical change is conceptually closest to Harvard Professor Clayton Christensen's definition of disruptive change. We consider creative and intermediating change similarly disruptive. With these industry evolutions, value inherent in a business' assets and activities is undermined and can migrate to new players.

A look at the trajectory of Australian industries highlights that about 60 per cent can expect significant disruption over the coming decade (see figure 15).

Note, however, that the positioning of industries in this figure represents an averaged view. The key drivers of disruption we see affecting industries are not just changes in technology (though changes such as more universal broadband, big data and analytics, 3D printing, robotics, and further inroads in biotechnology will have a significant impact), but also changing consumer attitudes accentuated and accelerated by social media, regulation such as the financial services industry enquiry and other legislation to adjust to changing industry

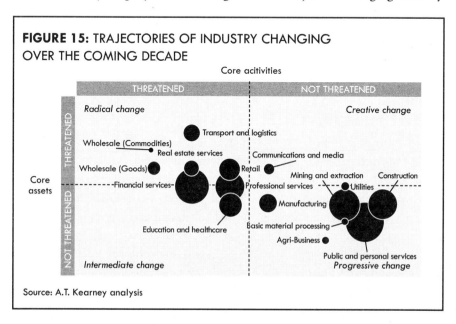

FIGURE 15: TRAJECTORIES OF INDUSTRY CHANGING OVER THE COMING DECADE

Source: A.T. Kearney analysis

conditions, as well as further globalisation. How these play out by sector and sub-sector will differ. The communications and media industry, for example, is made up of broadcast and print media, both facing radical change. The fixed line communications sector is facing creative change, as the National Broadband Network makes existing assets obsolete. The information and communications technology services sector is facing intermediating change as the industry's core activities of integrating and managing proprietary IT solutions is transformed by cloud services. The mobile communications sector is also facing more progressive change as 4G services are rolled out.

Core activities in most industries are vulnerable, as digital technologies are driving down transaction costs, making it easier and more efficient for suppliers to reach customers, such as automobile and other manufacturers that are bypassing dealerships to reach customers. It is also becoming easier for businesses to reconfigure themselves to focus on value-creating activities and outsourcing those that may be core but are not differentiating and hence will not drive longer-term value. Addressing disruption head on will be vital for long-term survival and success.

THE BARRIERS TO ADDRESSING DISRUPTIVE CHANGE

In many ways, business' current formula for success makes responding to disruption difficult. The focus on sustaining competitive advantage is logical for most organisations. What makes businesses great is their ability to optimise resource deployment and processes to outperform competitors as they deliver value propositions with a well-defined profit formula. Stability is the enemy when facing industry disruption.

A review of businesses that have failed to respond to industry disruptions points to four root causes:

COGNITION PATTERNS

Most people and companies apply biases or mental models in an attempt to capture institutional knowledge and experience to support decision making and efficiency. While this may be efficient, it narrows perspective and impedes agility, as we will explore in chapter five. Biases, defined as a deviation from rational judgements or behaviours, exist everywhere. Decision making is influenced by a wide range of well-researched biases that nevertheless remain widespread. Much of this is unconscious, some arising from practices that have underpinned past successes and others not necessarily constructive. With confirmation bias, for example, managers tend to favour evidence that confirms, rather than challenges, prevailing thinking. Similarly, they can filter or limit information in communications with more senior executives to win sought-after confirmation. How arguments are anchored or framed has a big impact on a decision's outcome. We also tend to value avoided losses more than received gains, and we overestimate the prevalence of recent or vivid, easily-imagined events.

Knowledge structures derived from past experiences can lock executives into seeing the world in a particular way. Consequently, many companies maintain business models that they believe will achieve profits but actually limit new opportunities. As a result, responding to change is difficult. An example of this behaviour is U.S. typewriter manufacturer Smith Corona, which in 1985 believed the answer to competing with the growing popularity of personal computers (PCs) was to introduce a word processor and a typewriter with an electronic spelling function. The company finally introduced a PC of its own in 1991 with partner Acer Computers. However, senior executives did not really believe in the product and discontinued it shortly after launch. Smith Corona's CEO continued to believe there was a strong market for the company's core products, and by 1995, the company had filed for bankruptcy.

STRUCTURAL INERTIA

Most organisation's capabilities are built on routines that allow them to execute tasks repeatedly, efficiently, reliably, and with little variation. Most processes are made up of thousands of smaller interlocking work practices. Inertia sets in because they do not change their routines automatically as the surrounding environment evolves, nor do they revise their business structure in kind. This affects a firm's adaptability.

IBM is a good example. The company reached dizzying heights of success by 1984, when it produced four Nobel Prize winners in physics whose breakthroughs in mathematics, memory storage, and telecommunications led IBM to make great strides in expanding computing capabilities. Yet less than a decade later, IBM posted a record-setting loss in American business at the time: $8 billion in 1993. The company had been slow to respond to a succession of industry changes, where the shift from mainframes to PCs had caused hardware costs to plummet and product development cycles to accelerate.

IBM did go through a corporate transformation during the industry shift, but the road was rough. IBM entered the PC market by forming an independent business unit that bypassed its long, internal product development cycles to embrace open standards. In this respect, it altered its structure. The company did not use its own chips and operating system, which were superior to the Intel chip and disk operating system (DOS), which was prevalent at the time. That fateful decision cleared the path for what would become the dominant Windows-Intel model. Despite the major misstep, IBM overcame inertia by steering away from the rapidly commoditising IT industry with a more balanced mix of high-value offerings:[48]

- Growing its services and software businesses through internal investments and acquisitions
- Acquiring more than 200 companies, at a cost of $30 billion, to fill out a portfolio of products and services in strategic growth areas, including analytics
- Divesting low-growth, low-margin product lines and technologies such as memory chips, technology components, printers, displays, and ultimately personal computers

Commenting on the divestments a few years ago, Bridget van Kralingen, general manager for IBM North America, said: "This was easier said than done, as those were technologies, products, and even whole markets that we had invented and developed".[49]

SHORT-TERMISM

Most organisations make decisions with a focus on the next one to three years, which is inadequate when planning for disruptive change. This was confirmed in a recent A.T. Kearney study where we found that about 60 per cent of organisations have a strategic planning horizon of three years or less. This is often aligned with the time period over which leadership incentives apply. An example is ANZ Bank's divestiture of Grindlays Bank in 2000. Grindlays had a reasonable business both in Asia and in emerging markets up until the 1990s, when it faced significant write-downs because of the Asian crisis and instability in Russia. These positions were forecast to recover in a relatively short period, but instead, the business was divested, much to the benefit of Standard Chartered Bank and Ashmore Group's Mark Coombs. In 2012, ANZ chief Mike Smith called the 2000 sale of its Grindlays India unit a big strategic mistake. "We have to start again," he said. "We will obviously invest more and build our business there".[50]

Fairfax Holdings Limited demonstrated a similar short-term orientation in 2000 when faced with the potential of acquiring Realestate.com.au and Carsales.com.au. When former Fairfax chief Fred Hilmer joined the firm in 1998, the board wanted a quick fix and had set a $40 million cost-cutting target, which he met.[51] Fairfax could have bought Realestate.com.au in 2000 and again

KODAK IN THE CROSSHAIRS

The demise of Kodak is a familiar example that illustrates cognitive bias, structural inertia, and short-termism.

Kodak was a chemicals company, making most of its money from analogue film. It followed the so-called razor-blade business model, selling cameras at a low price, sometimes even at a loss, in order to sell the complementary consumable product: analogue film.

The emergence of new competition from digital technology meant consumers replaced their analogue cameras with digital ones, which these days are being replaced by mobile phones. With its eye off the ball, Kodak remained focused on its existing analogue business until the technology gap was no longer bridgeable and it was out of the picture. The 130-year-old photographic film pioneer had to file for bankruptcy and obtain a $950 million, 18-month credit facility from Citigroup to keep going. Does this scenario sound familiar?

While Kodak felt overwhelmed by change, our view is that Kodak had time to manage the transition from old to new but failed to navigate the industry disruption.

It is surprising to realise that Kodak invented the digital camera in 1975. Four years later, a former Kodak executive wrote a report on how analogue film would be replaced by digital by 2010. Even as the inventor of the technology, the company did not leverage it and instead clung to a cognitive bias of focusing on film and the underlying profit model. As a senior vice president of Kodak observed in The Wall Street Journal in 1985, "It is very hard to find anything (with profit margins) like colour photography that is legal".[53]

Structural inertia made it difficult for this industry leader to shake off old routines, such as product development processes that were more research-oriented than customer-centred or a head office bureaucracy rather set in its ways. Also, by 1996, when Casio and Sony had already launched their first digital cameras, Kodak was enjoying its peak year, with two-thirds of global market share and revenues of nearly $16 billion. This position led to short-termism. With a time horizon of one-to-three years, life looked good for Kodak. A longer view, however, may have enabled the company to predict and outwit what became inevitable.

in 2005 and Carsales.com.au in early 2000s but chose to avoid the dilution of short-term earnings. With the board's lack of focus on long-term growth, Fairfax failed to replicate its dominance in print classified ads by missing three opportunities to buy the top websites for home and car listings. Carsales' market capitalisation is now about 25 per cent larger than Fairfax's overall size, and Realesatate.com.au is similarly positioned.

THE X FACTOR

Finally, there are all of those factors outside an organisation's control that influence its ability to transform and thrive. These X factors, or wild cards, include global catastrophes, bad luck, incompetence, and disadvantages from industry structure or insurmountable differences in market power.

Think about the Internet browser wars back in the 1990s. Microsoft out-muscled Netscape by leveraging its existing PC distribution network. Microsoft Windows had more than a 90 per cent share of the desktop operating system market, and Microsoft's browser, Internet Explorer, was bundled with every copy of Windows. With customers having this browser by default, the company easily dominated market share. Sometimes there is nothing you can do if your competitor is powerful enough to outperform you. Netscape didn't make any strategic mistakes, so to speak, but as Jim Barksdale, president and CEO of Netscape Communications summarised, "Very few times in warfare have smaller forces overtaken bigger forces".[52] Regulatory action, forcing Microsoft to unbundle its browser from its operating system, came too late.

PREPARE TO OUTWIT DISRUPTION

Strategies that ensure a busines's longevity confront disruption before it occurs. Three moves can help prevent or overcome the root causes of failure in the face of change (see figure 16).

ADOPT A CHALLENGER'S MINDSET

In the mid-20th century, economist Joseph Schumpeter offered a view of creative destruction that seems truer now than ever. The balance between running a current business effectively versus creating new businesses to address future customer needs, and restructuring or exiting legacy businesses that may have peaked in value, is clearly shifting away from the status quo. A healthy disengagement from the core business is vital, as is awareness of any biases in mental models about the added value of the company's capabilities.

This is true whether you are leading or following in market share. Once a business succeeds, it has something to lose, so the focus shifts to preserving the status quo. Kevin Turner, chief operating officer of Microsoft, noted at a recent Microsoft Worldwide Partner Conference the need for a new mindset—a challenger's mindset. Microsoft still maintains nearly 90 per cent of PC operating system and core application sales, but the definition of the market is broadening if tablets, smartphones, and game consoles are added. In this context, Microsoft's market share is around 14 per cent, and it should think of itself as a challenger. The three themes Microsoft has chosen to focus on are disruption, differentiation, and speed—clearly a call to reappraise how the company is thinking about its business.

Standing back and assessing how your industry may evolve starts with confirming the definition of your market. What job do we really fulfil for our customers? With whom do we share buyers and suppliers? Jack Welch, the CEO of General Electric from 1991 to 2001, a period in which the company added nearly $500 billion in shareholder value, would exhort his executives to "redefine your market to one in which your share is no more than 10 per cent and grow".

Once you have defined the business you are in, consider your business as a portfolio of capabilities. This is a powerful way of breaking free from the typical view of a business as structured around product lines or customer segments to understand which assets and activities will underpin future success.

FIGURE 16: KEY THEMES FOR MANAGING CROSSHAIRS

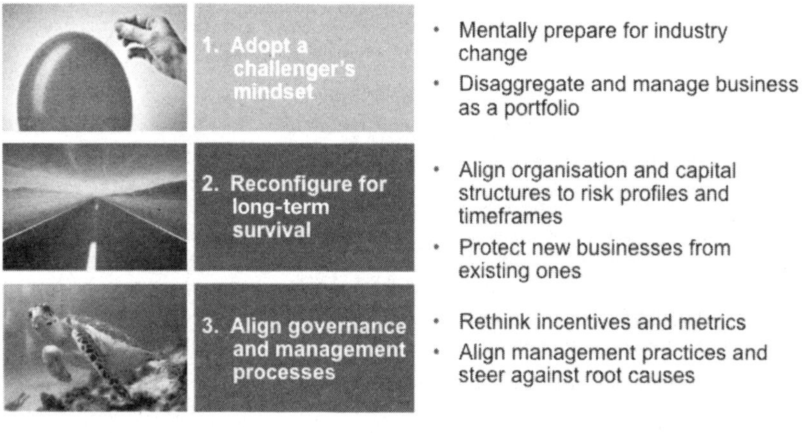

1. Adopt a challenger's mindset	• Mentally prepare for industry change • Disaggregate and manage business as a portfolio
2. Reconfigure for long-term survival	• Align organisation and capital structures to risk profiles and timeframes • Protect new businesses from existing ones
3. Align governance and management processes	• Rethink incentives and metrics • Align management practices and steer against root causes

Source: A.T. Kearney analysis

Disaggregating the business into capabilities, and considering the current and future value of all key assets and core activities a company performs, can provide a clear view of several things: the capabilities the business should bet on for the future, which may have peaked in value that should be discontinued or divested, and where the business can leverage its assets and activities differently to drive future value. Considering your business as a portfolio of capabilities and plotting them against an asset-activities matrix provides a useful guide for strategic decision making and resource allocation (see figure 17). With the refined understanding of the market, you can now assess several points: What customer needs do the defined capabilities fulfil? How might the need be otherwise addressed? Which will be substituted, which fulfilled better with different assets or activities, and which remain valuable for the future?

Against this backdrop, the broad strategies for the parts of the business become apparent. Legacy capabilities threatened with obsolescence should be run for efficiency, with the business scaling back, divesting, or closing down the activities as their value declines. Capabilities built around key assets with future value, but for which core processes or governance practices are threatened with obsolescence, should be repurposed, leveraging the assets to drive new value for customers, such as moving bricks-and-mortar retail from shops to showrooms as online buying grows. Capabilities based on activities with clear future value, but for which the

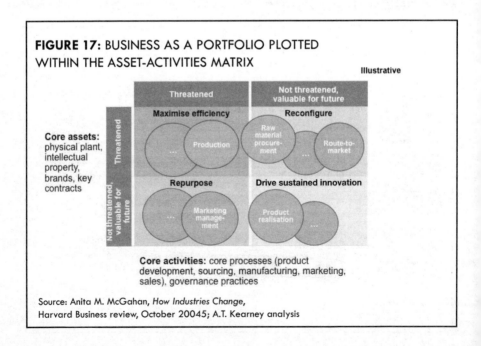

FIGURE 17: BUSINESS AS A PORTFOLIO PLOTTED WITHIN THE ASSET-ACTIVITIES MATRIX

Illustrative

Source: Anita M. McGahan, *How Industries Change*, Harvard Business review, October 20045; A.T. Kearney analysis

FUJIFILM SEES THE BIG PICTURE

Fujifilm is an interesting contrast to Kodak, illustrating how viewing a business as a portfolio can lead to a new strategic perspective. Although both firms realised photography would be going digital in the 2000s, they differed in their diversification and execution. Fujifilm's success hinged on a few key moves: in-house innovation, a joint venture with American printer manufacturer Xerox, and flexibility in applying its technologies in new areas, such as cosmetics.

If we examine Fujifilm's case against the asset-activity matrix, we see that the company eluded the crosshairs of disruption with a clear strategy and tenacious execution (see figure). They distinguished R&D as their core activity, together with their strong portfolio of chemicals, patents, and expertise in films as their core assets, and took these with them on their journey to the future.

Of course, Fujifilm had to let go of some things as part of this transition. The company cashed out its manufacturing facilities, realising they were neither a core activity nor a core asset. Fujifilm also transformed its printing business model by installing kiosks to print digital photos using their in-house technology, whereas Kodak needed a partner firm to make this possible.

FUJIFILM EXAMPLE: ASSET-ACTIVITIES MATRIX

Core activities

	Threatened	Not threatened, valuable for future
Threatened (Core assets)	**Film—manufacturing** **Core assets:** Manufacturing facilities **Core activities:** Producing films at the lowest costs **Action:** Manage decline and cash-out. Fujifilm closed down manufacturing facilities and managed their assets before they became liabilities	**Film—product development** **Core assets:** Product knowledge, prototyping facilities, relationship with buyers **Core activities:** Developing optical films—prototyping, developing, testing **Action:** Acquire and merge to obtain LCD film product development expertise
Not threatened, valuable for future (Core assets)	**Film—printing** **Core assets:** (Digital) film printing technologies, relationship with buyers **Core activities:** Printing pictures from film **Action:** Transform business model—leverage assets and restructure relationship with buyers; Fujifilm used digital printing technology and installed kiosk digital printers and produced home digital printers	**Research and development** **Core assets:** Strong portfolio of chemicals, patents, and expertise in films **Core activities:** Developing new materials and techniques **Action:** Incubate and diversify using assets—experiment and develop new skills and products; Fujifilm launched a skincare product

Source: A.T. Kearney analysis

underlying assets are threatened, should be reconfigured. For example, a pharmaceutical company could acquire intellectual property in a new treatment area to support its new product development or distribution capabilities, or seek out new customers when existing segments become saturated. Finally, capabilities that have future value should be managed for maximum effectiveness, providing the focus for sustaining innovations to drive further differentiation and advantage.

RECONFIGURE FOR LONG-TERM SURVIVAL

Stability is vital when managing large organisations. Company, business-unit, and organisational structures are set up and supported with a wide range of systems for finance, human resources, information, and other functions. Therefore, flexible reconfiguration is difficult but no less important. Areas of new opportunity typically require different management approaches. For instance, new businesses benefit from a model based on trial and error, where small wins and inexpensive or early failures are permitted. In established businesses, the management models should be efficient, consistent, established, and supported by transformation programs to drive improvements and change.

Firms that can navigate disruptions also take a fit-for-purpose, flexible approach to their capital structure. In line with portfolio components, capabilities can be characterised in terms of cash flow stability, distinguishing more mature, stable funding requirements from riskier growth investments. Flexibility helps align investors' different time horizons and risk preferences while giving them access to various entities. This in turn should make the firm more agile and increase the responsiveness to a changing industry environment, positioning the company for long-term survival.

ALIGN GOVERNANCE AND MANAGEMENT PROCESSES

Support long-term vision and a challenger's mindset with a review of leadership incentives that are balanced between short-term returns and the chances for long-term survival. Align measures of success with the time horizon for expected returns, which can correlate with investor expectations. For instance, reward risk-taking and innovation if it is a high-risk and high-return initiative. Reward optimised revenue and cost balance if the initiative involves bond-like cash flow. In any case, it can help to accept earnings volatility rather than stifle critical investments.

Commonly used, conventional metrics to measure project success and return, such as net present value (NPV), real options, or hurdle rates have their limitations. For instance, hurdle rates tend to create a bias towards short-term, quick payoff projects because they severely penalise project benefits that occur in the longer term. Similarly, NPV calculations are as good as the accuracy of the discount rate assumed. A small increase or decrease in the rate will have a considerable effect on the final output. These measures can be useful starting points to value investments, but they certainly do not provide definitive answers on which executives can rely for all investment decisions.

Finally, think about fostering a culture of innovation by setting aside funds and resources for experimentation. Innovation can be managed by aligning it with different portfolio requirements. People from diverse backgrounds can support that innovation with their new perspectives and mental models. At Google, one of the world's innovation leaders, employees can devote 20 per cent of their time to work on projects of their own choosing. Moreover, Google does not track how employees spend their time. This 20-80 idea functions more as a philosophy—where new projects are brought to the table by whomever has the most innovative ideas, not just by people at the top of the hierarchy. Google has based its culture on this approach, and it is paying off. Gmail, Google AdSense, and Google News are examples of major service offerings initiated by self-motivated Google employees.

TAKE AIM AT DISRUPTION

If firms are prepared for the fight, they can manage the conflict that comes with the disruption that is inevitable in most industries. In the near term, industries that are prone to technological changes, such as information and communications, media, marketing, and those that deal directly with changing customer needs and expectations (such as retail, financial services, and professional services) are most exposed. In the longer term, beyond five to seven years, most public-service sectors are likely to be similarly upended, including education, government, utilities, health, and transport. Other sectors such as accommodation, construction, and mining are not immune, though pressures may come mainly from competitors aggressively driving sustaining innovations.

So where do you start? Stand back, and assess where your industry is headed and the market in which you compete. Disaggregate your business, and evaluate which assets and activities will drive future value and which to reconfigure to support your next-generation business model. Taking this broader approach to strategic planning is worthwhile and necessary for businesses to survive into the next generation. Reconfiguring the business for long-term survival and aligning the organisation, governance, and management processes for greater agility are addressed in the next chapter—where we explore what it takes for a company to be truly agile.

CHAPTER 5

BE AGILE

AGILITY AS A NECESSITY

I n the preceding chapters we outlined the dynamic business environment and strategic challenges Australian businesses will face over the next 20 years. While predicting the exact impact of those changes is tricky, we are certain of this: Businesses will need to become more nimble and responsive to cope with the challenges and capture the opportunities. In short, they will need to be agile.

Research confirms a direct correlation between agility and business performance. In a 2009 survey by the Economist Intelligence Unit, nearly 90 per cent of 400 senior executives reported believing that organisational agility is crucial for business success but admitted they were not agile enough.[54] This is particularly pertinent for Australian businesses, which are exposed to three factors:

- **Twenty years of success.** The financial crisis has not been felt in Australia with anything like the intensity with which it struck the United States and Europe. As a result, managers have not had to rethink their operating models or find new markets as a matter of survival. With such a long period of success and uninterrupted growth, businesses in this Lucky Country have limited experience with crisis and are more inclined to stick with current business models. Over time, this may have made them complacent and resistant to change.

- **Demanding directors' obligations.** Board members in Australia face unlimited personal liability. For every decision they make, they incur the risks from multiple interpretations of Corporations Act 2001 principles, such as duty of good faith, improper use of position or information, or acting in the best interest of companies. There also are numerous other legal responsibilities on diverse areas such as health, safety, environment, and worker compensation. This regulatory landscape, and the complexity of our business environment, can lead to a shorter-term strategic horizon and behaviour from executives.

- **A culture of conformity.** Interestingly, Australia is among the most risk-averse countries within the Organisation for Economic Co-operation and Development (OECD) based on econometrics such as private R&D, percentage of entrepreneurs in the population, state welfare, and barriers to competition.[55] Conformity is a cultural watchword as behavioural studies suggest a low-risk attitude in Australia.[56] Change is not necessarily embraced nor sought. Agility may therefore be undervalued in a culture that is, at times, inclined to the status quo.

What is the enemy within your firm? Defeating this enemy is essential for another 20 years of success. At the dawn of important changes, three Australian characteristics are defining the enemy within: resistance to change, conformity, and the complexity of our businesses. However, you personally visualise or experience it for your business—be it the burdensome load, the hurdle to overcome, the shackles to break, or all three—it is important to be nimble, cope with the challenges, and capture future opportunities. To become truly agile, the enemy within must be overcome.

DEFINING AGILITY

The word agile, from the Latin word *agilis*, comes from the Latin verb *ago*, meaning "to do, act, or move". For an organisation, being agile can be defined as a capability that involves focus, strength, adaptability, and speed of response. However capability is more than a skill set or an ability to change and react. Agility also can be seen as a mindset embedded in the company's culture. It becomes a natural way to be—a force of habit—rather than a series of one-off efforts to adapt to a given disruption. In other words, agility can be defined as the capability and cultural mindset that enables an organisation to lead in dynamic conditions and implement change as a matter of routine towards a distinct purpose.

So, what enables agility in our fast-evolving environment? This chapter aims to provide a framework to understand what it means to be agile.

Agility requires persistence and determination to keep the organisation in motion. There is no obvious solution or single answer for this capability, but rather three ingredients that, when combined, create the recipe for agility (see figure 18).

Each ingredient addresses one of the specific challenges faced by Australian businesses:

Purpose. An agile organisation knows its purpose as well as where its competitive advantage lies. It engages the workforce through inspirational leaders and remains flexible and creative without losing focus on its main purpose,

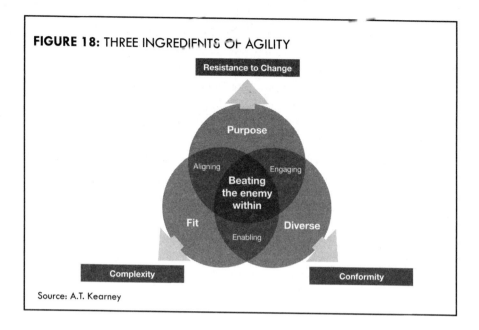

FIGURE 18: THREE INGREDIENTS OF AGILITY

Resistance to Change

Purpose

Aligning

Engaging

Beating
the enemy
within

Fit

Diverse

Enabling

Complexity

Conformity

Source: A.T. Kearney

which motivates and compels people. Resistance to change is avoided by having a clear purpose and communicating how any changes align to, and build upon, that purpose to ensure people understand and can rally around the change.

Fit. To remove complexity, a lean and simple operating model is crucial and creates organisational strength. Aligning the building blocks of the operating model creates the ability to respond to market dynamics quickly and achieve the agile outcome.

Diverse. To tackle the challenge of internal biases and conformity, social, cognitive, and attitudinal diversity is key. Being able to attract and retain a diverse talent pool can bring new ideas, foster innovations, suggest alternative paths to solve issues, and open up new management styles.

PURPOSE

In our experience, companies face two main challenges while attempting to create a deep sense of purpose that can diffuse through all levels of the organisation.

Lack of top-down direction. The first challenge lies in the short-term focus of both leadership and shareholders. On one hand, executives, having led a company through past growth and success, tend to rest on their laurels and stick with those success formulas. On the other hand, analysts, shareholders, and leaders often measure success based on metrics that favour short-term results and meeting forecasts rather than setting a more meaningful, long-term direction.

Absence of bottom-up involvement. Agility is powered through an engaged and passionate organisation. We still see employees who don't understand how their roles fit into the bigger picture. Passion and entrepreneurship tend to be stifled by cumbersome governance processes. Any reference to change and transformation elicits negativity, with previous transformation efforts generally focusing on cost-cutting and lacking effective change agents within the business. As a result, past less-than-successful attempts "prove" that transformation is neither required nor useful, lowering engagement further.

Agility springs from aligning leadership and staff on a common purpose. An agreed and relentless focus on a meaningful goal, with an engaged workforce, supported by inspired leadership, can establish the basis for a distinct capability for agility. Creating such a purposeful organisation requires three characteristics:

FOCUS ON A MEANINGFUL GOAL

In a *Harvard Business Review* paper, authors Nick Craig and Scott Snook say purpose is a "key to navigating the complex world we face today, where strategy is ever changing and few decisions are obviously right or wrong".[57] However, they say fewer leaders have a strong sense of their own leadership purpose or action plan to make it come true and thus often fail to achieve their most ambitious target. To be agile, a company must articulate the purpose and goal that set the foundation for its distinct capabilities.

A meaningful goal has to combine three qualities. First, it must be *inspirational* by providing a clear answer to why it represents the company's objective, what success looks like, and why it is compelling and exciting. Second, it should be *ambitious* and show that the benefits of success are substantial. Finally, it should be *attainable* to sustain motivation and provide a clear path in which the workforce can have confidence.

This translates into a distinct capability that enables an organisation to deliver its value proposition for customers and employees, prioritise investments, and attract people who believe in the same purpose.

Uncovering a company's meaningful purpose is no easy task, as it involves revising or rearticulating the historical core value proposition. It requires introspection and answering the following questions posed by management consultant Peter Drucker: What business are you in? Who are your customers? What do they value? With whom do you compete? What are you really good at?[58] For instance, a mortgage company could redefine its meaningful purpose from "the number one mortgage company in Australia" to "helping people buy their dream home". Once redefined, a meaningful purpose helps the company think more expansively and better anticipate and respond to external trends.

BUILDING SUPPORTIVE, INSPIRED LEADERSHIP

Leaders have a key role in articulating the company's purpose and instilling it throughout the organisation. Elon Musk—co-founder of PayPal, SpaceX, and Tesla Motors—emphasises the need for a leader to keep a clear vision of where the company is heading, to embrace fully the "why" of the company. This purpose ties leadership and the organisation together.

Inspired and inspiring leaders have foresight and are willing to act to deliver on their purpose. Their purpose is visible to others, and it makes their actions—the change—worthwhile. These leaders have the courage to withdraw outdated strategies, while simultaneously avoiding drag-and-drop models and biases derived from past experience or conventional metrics. They are men and women who are able to face and prepare themselves not only for the realities of today, but also for the uncertainties of tomorrow, and they bring their people with them on the journey.

They do so through developing relationships with people who are very different from themselves, recognising the benefits of diverse networks in identifying new patterns and solutions. This could take the form of leader networks at different operational levels that are spaces for sharing learning and achieving operational alignment.

More importantly, inspired leaders have the courage to take risks when they have built up a strong conviction and have the emotional stamina to go forward with their ideas, even when discouraged by other people.

Being a leader in an agile organisation requires long-term focus, while simultaneously engendering a sense of urgency and commitment to end goals.

FOSTERING AN ENGAGED WORKFORCE

An engaged workforce is essential to deliver the meaningful goal of the company. It means the business is well-connected internally and has the capability to work as a unified force towards a goal. In our experience, successful transformations typically over-invest in the workforce and reach a tipping point, thanks to key influencers and large-scale employee involvement. This environment typically has four characteristics:

- **Employees have a strong personal sense of purpose** that is aligned to the company's purpose. In other words, the workforce feels part of a cause that goes beyond the boundaries of their immediate role.

GOOGLE: A CASE STUDY IN AGILITY THROUGH PURPOSE

Many companies claim to have a clear sense of purpose, but how many share a powerful one? In most instances, the purpose is articulated around customer centricity and creation of shareholder value. For both top management and the workforce, this can hardly sound differentiating and is difficult to identify with.

Google's stated purpose, on the other hand, is a good example of what a powerful purpose looks like:

Organise the world's information and make it universally accessible and useful.

This purpose provides a clear direction without being too restrictive. It focuses on the end, not the means. It opens up degrees of freedom to stimulate employees' imagination and creativity. With such a purpose, Google expanded its business well beyond a search engine on the Web to become a multi-faceted company. During the past decade, Google has:

- Developed more than 300 products including Gmail, Google Talk, Google Maps, Picasa, and Google Apps
- Benefited from empowered employees, pioneering the 20-80 rule, which allows them to spend time on personal projects
- Sustained annual double-digit growth

- **Employees can communicate openly.** They have the freedom to nurture and grow their network continually, access and share expert knowledge, and are both given the time and rewarded appropriately for initiatives that contribute to an agile organisation.
- **The organisational culture is entrepreneurial and open to change** at all levels. It does not perceive transformation as a separate, one-off effort led by external teams but sees it as the norm and led by internal teams.
- **Leaders demonstrate confidence by giving employees opportunities** for early involvement through staff-level participation in discussion groups, trials, and pilots. They shape behaviours, create early adopters and champions, and hold employees accountable for their part in the transformation.

FIT

Being agile requires a second ingredient—what we call a Fit Transformation™ operating model—that will enable the organisation to swiftly manoeuvre in anticipation of emerging threats and opportunities.

Fitness comes with a challenge. As organisations succeed and grow, they add resources and leadership layers and put protocols in place. This often leads to cluttered, clumsy, and complex operations. Activities are often spread across business units, with unclear responsibilities and accountabilities. Duplicate roles arise, particularly transactional ones, as businesses grow and the organisation fails to optimise along the way. Furthermore, governance is often based on outdated processes derived from existing capabilities and success measures tailored for yesterday's reality, rather than tomorrow's challenges.

Many companies attempt to lead transformation through ruthless cost-cutting, growing so lean that they become weak and unresponsive. Companies are complex, living organisms. Like the human body, they are subject to imbalances. Just as a thyroid disorder can impact a range of bodily functions, an intervention in one area of an organisation requires careful consideration of interconnections with many other parts of the business, which must be carefully identified and evaluated.

While stripping out costs is often necessary to eliminate non-value-adding structures and processes, it is, in itself, insufficient for becoming fit—just as going on a stringent diet that limits nutrients and does not include exercise will make you frail and vulnerable instead of physically fit. A fit organisation balances leanness with strength and flexibility (see figure 19).

Three steps help businesses achieve a balance between strength, flexibility, and leanness:

FIGURE 19: BALANCING STRENGTH, FLEXIBILITY, AND LEANNESS

Strong	Flexible	Lean
	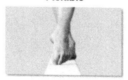	
Deep capabilities	**Market responsiveness**	**Cost advantage and simplicity**
• What capabilities **differentiate** us • Which capabilities should be **strengthened**? • Where do we need to invest in and better retain **talent**?	• How do we foresee and embed deep **customer insights**? • How is our business nimble to respond to **market changes**? • How do we best **flex our resources or workforce**?	• Is our operating **model designed for purpose**? • How do we right-size and play to our **strengths**? • What are appropriate **cost/value tradeoffs** to drive simplicity and support our strategy?

Source: A.T. Kearney

1. TRANSLATE A PURPOSE INTO AN ALIGNED OPERATING MODEL

A.T. Kearney developed the Fit Transformation framework to translate strategy into an aligned operating model, embedded through comprehensive, grounded change management (see figure 20).

A.T. Kearney's approach includes two vital aspects of organisation transformation that are often neglected:

- **Balanced translation.** A Fit Transformation starts with the strategy—the meaningful purpose of the organisation. Many businesses attempt to design their new organisational structure without understanding what their business is trying to achieve. Without a purpose and its translation into an operating model, companies risk falling into a vicious cycle, changing their structure every two or three years. After identifying your purpose, identify the sources of value that will help the business achieve its goals. The next step is to draw out the implications for each of the operating model building blocks. Balanced translation turns the meaningful purpose into the

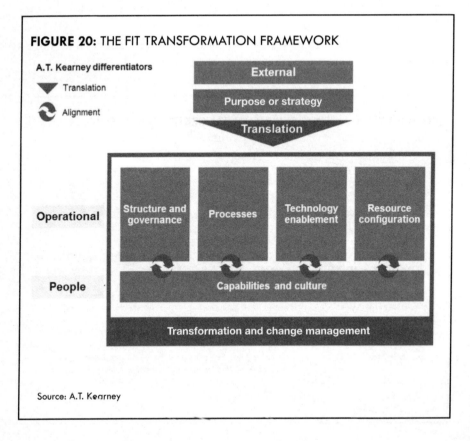

FIGURE 20: THE FIT TRANSFORMATION FRAMEWORK

Source: A.T. Kearney

right combination of organisational strength, agility, and cost to ensure it focuses on only the necessary elements. It is crucial to spend the time to gain the necessary insights and go through these steps thoroughly. Short-cuts in translation can lead to a scope that is too narrow, or conversely, so wide that it is overwhelming.

- **Holistic alignment.** This step uncovers and addresses misalignment in the operating model to shift performance structurally. Ideally, the model's building blocks align with one another. For instance, resource reconfig-uration decisions (such as geographic footprint, shared services models, and outsourcing) consider not only costs, but also the impact on customer experience in line with the company's customer service strategy, among other things. While reviewing cross-functional processes, consider gover-nance issues to ensure accountabilities remain transparent. Align across functions as well, to break down silos in the process. This can be achieved through cross-functional workshops and targets, and further down the road, through various mechanisms such as job rotation programs, team goals, and governance systems.

2. FINE-TUNE THE OPERATING MODEL FOR NIMBLENESS
Once aligned, the operating model's building blocks are adjusted to be nimble and agile (see figure 21).

- **Structure and governance** are relatively simple with clear accountabilities and built to harness specific strength.[59] Governance is oriented towards movement and progress, not only control. It focuses on taking key stra-tegic decisions and communicating them well—adopting a willingness to say no.
- **Processes** lead to end-to-end thinking and accountabilities. Performance management rewards risk taking and team accomplishments.
- **Technology enablement** delivers maximum value to the business through automated processes and efficient data mining and analysis.
- **Resource configuration** determines trade-offs and achieves optimal bal-ance between scale and focus, specialist and generalist roles, and a mix of internal versus external resources. It exploits regional or global centres of scale for purely transactional activities and includes a lean and efficient shared-service model offering high-quality, low-cost services to business units.
- **Capabilities and culture** mean that individuals and teams are engaged, need minimal self-orientation, and are working to a common purpose. Success measures are redefined to drive key capability development in the right places.

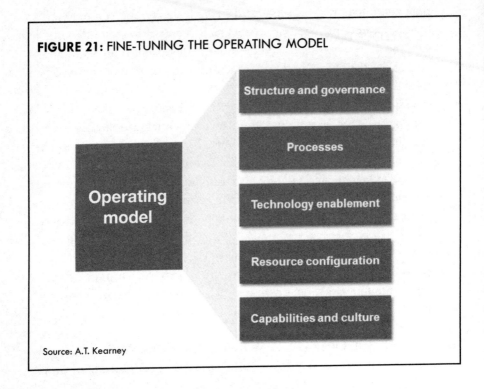

FIGURE 21: FINE-TUNING THE OPERATING MODEL

Operating model

Structure and governance

Processes

Technology enablement

Resource configuration

Capabilities and culture

Source: A.T. Kearney

3. MAKE CHANGE A MATTER OF ROUTINE: MANAGE THE TRANSFORMATION

The ideal organisational structure, processes, and governance achieve results when the behaviours of individuals change. A holistic change-management approach that engages, empowers, and gives ownership to people is essential for embedding agility into the organisation.

The approach comprises four dimensions to spur and embed change (see figure 22).

- **Spread or set direction.** This dimension gets the organisation's attention and sets the direction and need for change. Senior executives develop and communicate a clear vision and compelling case for change, organise the effort, assign resources, and oversee the results. Their involvement is visible and hands-on.

- **Shift or gain ownership.** Next, the sense of responsibility for achieving change shifts to individuals throughout the company by making them feel part of the process. Often, this means skipping a tell-and-teach process, instead bringing people in early to invest them, both emotionally and professionally, in the transformation.

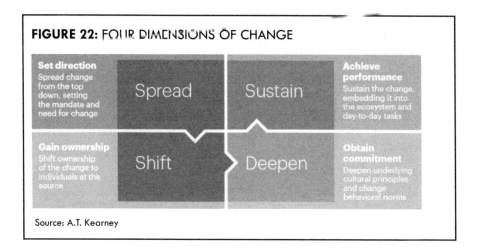

FIGURE 22: FOUR DIMENSIONS OF CHANGE

| Set direction
Spread change from the top down, setting the mandate and need for change | Spread | Sustain | Achieve performance
Sustain the change, embedding it into the ecosystem and day-to-day tasks |
| Gain ownership
Shift ownership of the change to individuals at the source | Shift | Deepen | Obtain commitment
Deepen underlying cultural principles and change behavioral norms |

Source: A.T. Kearney

- **Deepen or obtain commitment.** In parallel, people's attitudes and behaviour modify, not just in the way they perform specific tasks, but towards a true, emotional commitment to the change. The most effective way to achieve this is to invest significant time and effort in understanding what generates staff's commitment and what they need from the organisation to succeed. Fit Transformation employs a number of interventions and tactics to bring about behavioural shifts, such as cultural assessments and informal network analysis, and manages the softer elements that ensure change is more than skin deep.
- **Sustain or achieve performance.** Finally, an ecosystem and controls are firmly implanted in the company so that transformation takes root. Program funding shifts into the normal budgeting process, continuous improvement methodologies are implemented, and long-term outcomes are monitored.

When done well, change management endows the entire organisation with self-replicating capabilities that extend change far beyond completion of the immediate transformation program.

DIVERSE

Achieving a meaningful purpose and sustaining a Fit Transformation operating model requires a workforce that generates more and broader points of view. Yet we all know that organisations can be prone to bias, either conscious or unconscious. The most widespread examples of bias in decision making are:

- **Confirmation bias:** when only similar arguments are raised in conversation and in working groups

- **Group polarisation:** the tendency to make more extreme decisions if only a single opinion is voiced
- **The common knowledge effect:** a discussion focussed only on information that is commonly known, ignoring new or unique information known by a minority group

This is where corporate diversity can be a powerful tool to overcome biases. Organisations tend to limit diversity to race and gender, but true diversity encompasses an array of aspects (see figure 23).

Each dimension is used to characterise employees' attributes and answer a particular question:

PRACTICAL TOOLKIT: USING A DRIVE FRAMEWORK

The DRIVE framework—decide, recommend, input, veto, educate—defines decision-making rights, which is essential for managing a transformation. It helps channel decisions to the right level, identifying the people who are accountable for outcomes and outlining the expected behaviours.

A.T. Kearney used the DRIVE framework to align the roles and decision rights of a company's board and senior leadership team. In a nine-month process, we analysed all financial, people, and strategic-planning processes and encompassed regular and episodic decisions. As a result, decision making was tested and updated.

The output included a DRIVE grid, process maps, limits of authority, and an enterprise calendar:

	ecide "The buck stops here"	ecommend "The do-er"	nput "In the loop"	eto "Can put the brakes on"	ducate "Kept in the picture"
Role description	• Makes decisions • Accountable for outcome	• Gather input, develops, recommendation, implement decisions	• Provide timely input prior to decision based on specialised knowledge	• Can overturn decisions	• Receives communications about decisions
Expectation	• Considers recommendations prior to decisions • Transparent decision making process • Specifies inputs and information needs	• Executes communication of decisions • Discloses inputs and issues to "D" • Maintains DRIVE audit trial	• Participates in an ongoing two-way communication • Provides feedback on decision-making process to improve effectiveness	• Rights defined for specific circumstances (e.g. risk) • Serves as an "appeal" for "R" • Not required to respond or act • Used very selectively	• Includes anyone who will be affected by actions and decisions • Receives one-way communication
Behaviours	• Set clear conditions of satisfaction to the recommender • Accepts consequences for poor decisions • Avoid line items vetoes	• Communicates recommendation to "D", "I's" and "E's" simultaneously • Makes rationale explicit • Actively seeks input	• Ensures "R" has necessary information • Efficient, doesn't bottleneck the process	• Communicate rationale, explaining additional factors that must be taken into consideration • Weighs ramification of the veto	• Maintains peripheral involvement • Escalates key information that may have crucial bearing on decision-making • Comfortable with not having inputs

- Relational: How does the person relate to others?
- Occupational: What does the person do?
- Societal: How does the person connect and relate to society?
- Physical: Who is the person and what do others think they see?
- Value: What does the person believe in?
- Cognitive: How does the person think and process information?

FIGURE 23

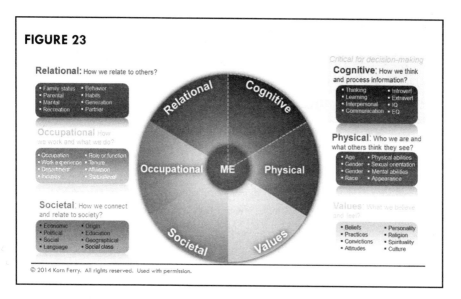

© 2014 Korn Ferry. All rights reserved. Used with permission.

Collectively, those dimensions can serve as a basis for assessing an organisation's level of diversity and define the right blend of diversity. A traditional benefit of diversity was to help create a workforce that reflects a changing customer base to understand and respond better to different customers' needs. Extending diversity to include a cognitive dimension can enrich the thoughts and ideas that are so essential to decision making for the future.

In recent decades, many scholars and researchers have studied the impact of workforce diversity on business performance and consistently shown an association between diversity and company performance. Two powerful benefits have been identified:

Higher returns. Studies conducted by Gallup and Harvard researchers demonstrated that diversity, engagement, and adaptive culture led to much better results, including growth of more than 39 per cent in higher customer satisfaction, 22 per cent in productivity, and 27 per cent in profitability.[60] Furthermore, the annual ranking of the most diverse companies produced by

DiversityInc reveals that, for five years, the stock index of companies ranking in the top 50 for diversity out-performed the S&P 500 by 80 per cent on total annualised return.[61]

Improved decision making. London Business School scholars compared socially similar and socially dissimilar groups while performing identical tasks, such as sharing information and taking business decisions.[62] They found significant evidence that diversity brings better decision making.

Despite the strengthening business case for diversity and some progress made during the past decade, most organisations are not fully diverse. Why is it still a work in progress? What prevents organisations from embracing diversity at all levels and through all dimensions?

THE UNCONSCIOUS BIAS

The paradox between diversity's acknowledged benefits and its apparent deficit in most organisations is best explained by one last and most entrenched factor: the unconscious bias. This is related to our implicit people preferences, formed by socialisation through our own experiences and our exposure to others' views about groups of people. Subjectivity, and the human tendency to generalise based on our view of ourselves, can create business risks because it impacts a company's assessment of its talent pool and the perception employees have of customers.

Helping employees become more aware of their own prejudices when interacting in the workplace is crucial to remove this internal, hidden barrier to diversity. Only when it is visible does it become possible to manage diversity proactively, turn it into a reality, and ultimately create an agile organisation.

READY TO BE AGILE

Beating the enemy within requires a balanced mix of the three ingredients for tackling specific obstacles in Australian companies:

- **Purpose.** A purposeful organisation vanquishes internal resistance to change.
- **Fitness.** A Fit Transformation operating model overcomes the complexity that organisations have created during their growth journey.
- **Diversity.** A diverse workforce addresses the challenges of conformity and organisational biases.

Each ingredient taken individually can deliver results, but combined, the recipe has the power to create a nimble and adaptive organisation—one that is

NOVARTIS: A CASE STUDY IN AGILITY THROUGH DIVERSITY

Novartis recognises that innovation is a crucial success factor for the pharmaceutical industry and that its own people should reflect the diversity of its customer base.

Early in 2006, Novartis started its journey to create a more diverse workforce, beginning with top management. The company is now at the top of the 2014 DiversityInc ranking and stands out with its strong board involvement in diversity issues. For instance:

- Seventy per cent of its international executives agree that diversity increases the quality of decisions.

- Thirty-two per cent of board members are not nationals of Switzerland, where the company has its headquarters.

Novartis uses diversity to become agile and outperforms its peer competitors on innovation metrics such as percentage of sales from new products. "Getting to this point has been a journey over almost a decade," company president Andre Wyss said in 2014. "We do this for a simple and powerful reason: we believe that diversity drives innovation, moves our business, and most importantly directly impacts our ability to develop lifesaving products and solutions".

truly agile. Because each ingredient influences the others, it is important to get the balance right. They are interdependent. A purposeful organisation is fit. Fitness and diversity nurture one another. Diversity and purpose reinforce the engaging organisation. The recipe takes a subtle hand to achieve but has the power to deliver significant results.

Once the organisation becomes confident in its agility, it can shift from reacting to provoking changes, thus challenging the status quo in a given market.

PART IV: LEAD THROUGH VALUE INNOVATION

CHAPTER 6

CREATE VALUE AT PIVOTAL CUSTOMER EVENTS

Customer centricity is today's rallying cry for companies that seek to stand out in a commoditising marketplace. Yet businesses across a broad spectrum of industries still lack the commitment and tools to deliver tangible improvements in the customer experience, much less shift their focus to create and harvest customer value systematically. Over the next 20 years, businesses with the ability to relate to customers on their own terms, and respond with services that truly meet their individual and collective needs, will reap huge rewards.

In this chapter, we share what A. T. Kearney calls pivotal customer events— an approach for prioritising what matters to the customer, aligning the organisation so it delivers outstanding customer experiences, and, in doing so, creating significant customer value. This approach is a reorientation away from conventional ways of becoming customer-centric towards a focus on creating customer value—a sustainable competitive advantage that will lead to long-term success.

RECOGNISING A PIVOTAL CUSTOMER EVENT

Customer events are meaningful commercial interactions that are important to a customer and generate an economic benefit for a business. These events comprise one or more moments of truth that a customer may experience across a transactional relationship in order to satisfy his or her objective or underlying need. For example, buying a first home is an incredibly important event. Within that event, however, getting the loan approved, having the documents signed, and settling on the house are all moments of truth. A customer will judge the event on the basis of the sum of these moments: nine right and just one wrong can severely disappoint.

Today, not making mistakes along the many customer events that exist is seen as a condition of doing business. Some call this "hygiene" or "business as usual", and organisations focus here on minimising complaints or detractors.

Building lasting positive customer relationships, on the other hand, requires successful resolutions based on deeper insights of customer needs and the broader role the customer's financial institution, phone carrier, utility company, or other service provider can play in addressing them. A shortlist of customer events that matter most to a large number of customers are called pivotal customer events. We use the word "pivotal" because these events can cut both ways. They are the transactions of greatest emotional importance between a customer and a service organisation and are a transactional inflection point where customer advocacy can be cemented or lost forever—an indicator of their significant potential either to create or destroy value.

Pivotal customer events are often triggered by a specific event, whether driven by the customer or by external forces, and focus on a specific customer goal. From the customer's perspective, they have a clear start and end point. Identifying pivotal customer events starts with developing a long list of all customer events and weighing their frequency of occurrence; importance to the customer; worth to the organisation (in revenue, profit, or value at risk); potential to anchor the relationship; and current performance to distil the five to 10 of greatest value to the customer and the business.

Focusing on five to 10 pivotal customer events is a more effective approach for developing customer centricity. Focusing on this shortlist of the most important events is a more efficient way to deploy improvement efforts. It also provides the basis for developing truly differentiated solutions aimed at creating real customer advocacy and customer value, rather than merely minimising detractors through a series of incremental improvements.

FROM TRANSACTION TO PIVOTAL CUSTOMER EVENT: A SIMPLE EXAMPLE

A wallet or handbag is an accessory most people take for granted—until it disappears. Its loss or theft impacts our lives on many levels. There is, of course, the immediate loss of cash and essential forms of identification, from a driver's licence to a healthcare card. And there's the loss of receipts and the less tangible, but sometimes more painful, loss of a treasured photo or keepsake. Finally, there is the loss of financial instruments—debit cards and credit cards—and the potential for loss of more money and identity. Add to this the time and place that this may have occurred (for example, on a night out, at a shopping mall, or on a business trip), and you can begin to imagine the state of distress that most people find themselves in when this happens.

Replacing a lost card is a one-dimensional, product-specific, and transactional approach to defining and solving this problem—yet this is the proposition that many banks offer their customers. Seeing the loss of the card as part of a larger loss—the wallet and everything it contains and represents—requires a multidimensional approach that is oriented to the true customer need. The lost wallet event is just one example of a reframe that can be powerful in focusing the organisation on what matters (see figure 24).

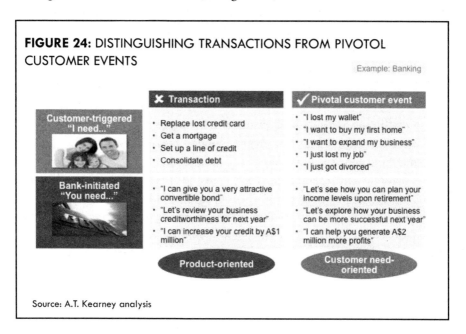

FIGURE 24: DISTINGUISHING TRANSACTIONS FROM PIVOTOL CUSTOMER EVENTS

Example: Banking

✖ Transaction	✔ Pivotal customer event
Customer-triggered "I need..." • Replace lost credit card • Get a mortgage • Set up a line of credit • Consolidate debt	• "I lost my wallet" • "I want to buy my first home" • "I want to expand my business" • "I just lost my job" • "I just got divorced"
Bank-initiated "You need..." • "I can give you a very attractive convertible bond" • "Let's review your business creditworthiness for next year" • "I can increase your credit by A$1 million"	• "Let's see how you can plan your income levels upon retirement" • "Let's explore how your business can be more successful next year" • "I can help you generate A$2 million more profits"
Product-oriented	Customer need-oriented

Source: A.T. Kearney analysis

How far should a bank go to solve what the customer sees as just one part of a larger problem? If you lose your credit card in Paris, a major credit card provider will ring a hotel or any restaurant you want to visit and guarantee payment on your behalf. Is this going too far? We don't think so. It lets customers keep going until they get their replacement card, ensures they continue to spend, and does not expose the provider to significant incremental risk.

Coming through for customers during these types of significant events opens up an opportunity to create the sort of advocacy and customer value of which service providers could otherwise only dream. This kind of advocacy hints at the deeper loyalty and value that can be created when a service provider understands and meets a customer's underlying needs.

WHAT IS WRONG WITH CUSTOMER-CENTRIC PROGRAMS?

Many service organisations invest heavily in customer-centric programs in the hope of improving the customer experience and, ultimately, boosting performance and returns. Nevertheless, few of these efforts ever get close to achieving their goals. In fact, many consume large amounts of effort and attention of frontline staff to the point that they lose focus and belief in the effort.

This problem has three root causes:

- **Activity over alignment.** Many customer experience initiatives often do not align or reinforce one another. A high volume of improvement projects can be a tell-tale indicator of ineffective activities.
- **Lack of understanding of customer needs.** Views can be inconsistent across the organisation as to what customers' problems are and what they value from a service provider.
- **Conflicting metrics and measures.** Customer satisfaction metrics that carry a lot of weight across the organisation may encourage actions that do not contribute meaningfully to business results.

Customer-centric efforts may feel good and are often accompanied by programs to raise employee engagement. Indeed, it is becoming more popular for executives to publicly commit to customer centricity. But reality is more complex than rhetoric, and it is a challenge to coordinate what are often disparate, and sometimes contradictory, efforts. Only one thing is certain: for most companies, the stakes have never been higher.

Pivotal customer events capture what is important to the customer and provide a logical way of organising priorities and aligning improvement efforts. This approach organises change activity, and ultimately the operating business, to help the organisation look at transactions and processes from a customer perspective in a way that builds loyalty and customer value.

FOUR PHASES TO ENGINEERING PIVOTAL CUSTOMER EVENTS

Engineering pivotal customer events involves four phases:

- **Discover** pivotal customer events.
- **Design** new solutions and mobilise the organisation.
- **Deliver** improvement outcomes in the form of practical solutions that can be rolled out on a large scale.
- **Sustain** the change by aligning expectations, culture, and behaviour to ensure that solutions last and that the organisation can adapt and evolve the customer experience as customer needs change (see figure 25).

Beyond being a robust methodology, one benefit of this approach is that it provides focus to align efforts to improve customer experience, prioritising what is

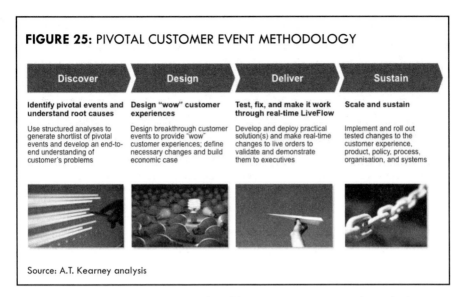

FIGURE 25: PIVOTAL CUSTOMER EVENT METHODOLOGY

Discover	Design	Deliver	Sustain
Identify pivotal events and understand root causes	**Design "wow" customer experiences**	**Test, fix, and make it work through real-time LiveFlow**	**Scale and sustain**
Use structured analyses to generate shortlist of pivotal events and develop an end-to-end understanding of customer's problems	Design breakthrough customer events to provide "wow" customer experiences; define necessary changes and build economic case	Develop and deploy practical solution(s) and make real-time changes to live orders to validate and demonstrate them to executives	Implement and roll out tested changes to the customer experience, product, policy, process, organisation, and systems

Source: A.T. Kearney analysis

most important to the customer and enabling a company to cut through the noise and distraction of what is typically a myriad of independent improvement efforts.

Let's look at each phase.

DISCOVER

What would happen if we were suddenly to start thinking more broadly about customer needs? It could be quite liberating or quite frightening, depending on how you see your role and the size of the commercial opportunity.

We need to align our businesses in ways that allow us to develop a rich, holistic understanding of our customers' top five to 10 events. Then we must ask ourselves if everything we do is really aligned with these needs.

Starting with the use of three analytical tools, the discover phase identifies those pivotal customer events that, if delivered seamlessly, will create lasting customer impressions and real value:

- **Segment insights** focuses on customer segments to retain, cross-sell to, or grow. The tool uses deep, structured interviews or facilitated discovery to identify the events in the life cycle that customers will remember. Those events that are most memorable to customers are likely to be the pivotal customer events.
- **Touch point analysis** assesses the frequency and criticality of customer interactions. Medium- to high-frequency and high-criticality touch points are likely to be signposts of pivotal customer events. The significance of these interactions may be because of their importance in meeting a cus-

tomer's underlying need or objective.

- **Friction point analysis** uses customer complaints data (including rebates and credits) to understand the frequency of issues and level of customer satisfaction. High-frequency, low-satisfaction interactions are likely to be part of a pivotal customer event. For example, mortgage settlements can generate significant complaints and be a highly visible point of failure during the home purchase episode.

Applying these tools allows an organisation to identify the most important episodes from the customer's perspective. A cross-functional think tank can be set up to engage and align the organisation and ensure that all relevant events are considered. Once the pivotal customer events have been identified, customer interviews and discovery surveys can be used to expose the root causes of customer dissatisfaction. Primary research can also provide a differentiated perspective and is key to developing real customer insights.

A portfolio of clearly understood and documented pivotal customer events should emerge from the discover phase. This analysis should clarify what causes customer pain and negatively influences customers' perspectives of the organisation today, and most importantly, the focal points of positive business-customer interaction that can leave a lasting impression in customers' minds tomorrow. You can—and should—forecast uplifts in net promoter scores or their equivalents if these pain points are correctly identified and addressed.

DESIGN

The changes that will deliver a compelling customer experience are crafted during the design phase. Put more simply, the design phase is about creating "wow" experiences that build customer advocacy and create customer value.

The desired changes to an event should be described using a set of targeted metrics—articulated both before and after transformation—and the episode should be tested to ensure that the design is future-proof.

The pivotal customer event needs to be engineered with a targeted customer and their specific needs taking centre stage. This requires a clear understanding of the five factors that combine to make a high-impact pivotal customer event:

- **Hear the voice of the customer.** Capture primary research to understand long-term customer needs and desires.
- **Measure critical-to-customer metrics.** Define critical metrics around customer effort, emotion, and cycle time. Benchmark performance against what could be possible in a world-class customer experience.

- **Demonstrate customer win themes.** Why should a customer choose us? Integrate strategy and brand positioning to develop winning themes. Ask the following questions: What do we want to be known for? How do we want our customers to describe us?

- **Use customer best practices.** Identify best practices and innovations from leading customer-centric industries, and integrate future digital capabilities to ensure convenience and flexibility in episode design.

- **Apply operational simplification.** Simplify end-to-end processes by defining sales, credit, operational, and other implications and by determining system and application requirements.

Remember that a properly designed customer event will not only improve the customer experience, but also make processes simpler and more efficient. Pivotal customer event engineering provides benefits to frontline workers and generates goodwill to support progress from one episode to the next.

A collaborative design phase can also create a team of advocates in the operational organisation that helps implement change. The new episode and its changes should be evaluated against 10 tests of a future-proof event design (see figure 26).

DELIVER

During the deliver phase, conceptual designs are transformed into tested and proven improvements. In other words, designs and theories are translated from

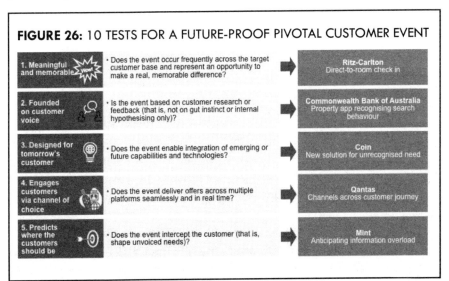

FIGURE 26: 10 TESTS FOR A FUTURE-PROOF PIVOTAL CUSTOMER EVENT

1. Meaningful and memorable	• Does the event occur frequently across the target customer base and represent an opportunity to make a real, memorable difference?	Ritz-Carlton Direct-to-room check in
2. Founded on customer voice	• Is the event based on customer research or feedback (that is, not on gut instinct or internal hypothesising only)?	Commonwealth Bank of Australia Property app recognising search behaviour
3. Designed for tomorrow's customer	• Does the event enable integration of emerging or future capabilities and technologies?	Coin New solution for unrecognised need
4. Engages customers via channel of choice	• Does the event deliver offers across multiple platforms seamlessly and in real time?	Qantas Channels across customer journey
5. Predicts where the customers should be	• Does the event intercept the customer (that is, shape unvoiced needs)?	Mint Anticipating information overload

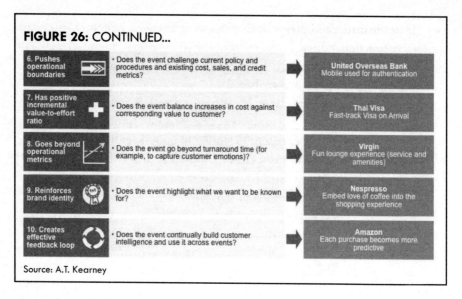

FIGURE 26: CONTINUED...

6. Pushes operational boundaries	• Does the event challenge current policy and procedures and existing cost, sales, and credit metrics?	**United Overseas Bank** Mobile used for authentication
7. Has positive incremental value-to-effort ratio	• Does the event balance increases in cost against corresponding value to customer?	**Thai Visa** Fast-track Visa on Arrival
8. Goes beyond operational metrics	• Does the event go beyond turnaround time (for example, to capture customer emotions)?	**Virgin** Fun lounge experience (service and amenities)
9. Reinforces brand identity	• Does the event highlight what we want to be known for?	**Nespresso** Embed love of coffee into the shopping experience
10. Creates effective feedback loop	• Does the event continually build customer intelligence and use it across events?	**Amazon** Each purchase becomes more predictive

Source: A.T. Kearney

PowerPoint into real-world processes, policies, and outcomes.

A.T. Kearney's LiveFlow methodology ensures effective implementation of the designed solutions by testing and fixing the agreed changes in real time and on live cases (see sidebar: The LiveFlow Methodology and Its Benefits). Live-Flow cuts through corporate cultural restraints and biases, but it doesn't turn the organisation upside down in the process.

The goal is to promote radical thinking—beginning by helping everyone understand the value of operating from a customer perspective and building a common perspective. That may mean taking a close look at metrics, internal structures, and traditional silo models that tend to pull business away from a customer-centric point of view.

SUSTAIN

This phase ensures that the organisation will make change last and adapt to emerging customer needs to remain competitive far into the future.

Institutionalising change is easier if the organisation is committed to improving the pivotal customer event, has top-down support, and enjoys aligned resources. Cultural change is reinforced by appointing end-to-end process owners for the event and including customer measures on all scorecards. Forward-thinking companies build a results-oriented culture that strives to delight customers and ruthlessly eliminates activities that do not create value for the customer (see figure 27).

The event owner's role has overriding importance. This should be someone who cares deeply about the ongoing quality of the customer experience and progress in the marketplace, is on the lookout for continual enhancements, and can resolve functional misalignments and competing priorities.

FIGURE 27: KEYS TO SUCCESSFULLY EXTEND PIVOTAL CUSTOMER EVENT THINKING ACROSS THE ORGANISATION

Internal alignment on clearly articulated goals and benefits, based on content-heavy top-down planning

Measurement of both performance and value, including churn and multi-product relationships

Systems thinking, based on mapping and managing the entire ecosystem

Governance over departments, grounded in top-down executive mandate and visibility for the program

Expert support to reinforce evolving attitudes towards change

On-the-ground operational support to identify and address issues on the spot

Source: A.T. Kearney

Customer segment owners are often the most logical owners of this role. In some cases, there may be events that align better to key products, and in those cases, product owners may be a better choice. In either case, whoever assumes the role is accepting a lot more responsibility and needs much more clout across the entire organisation than they have today.

One of the keys to effective execution—absent clear scale benefits from functional specialisation—is to adjust delivery team boundaries so that as much of the end-to-end process as possible is within (or accountable to) a single team. This promotes richer customer understanding and staff empathy for a pivotal customer event and for customers themselves. In cases where one team supports multiple events, delivery must be supported by a focus on targeted customer service outcomes, tailored scripting, and aligned policies, forms, and templates—tools that become guiderails to support desired behavioural changes.

Another effective tactic is to nurture distributed leadership from pivotal customer event champions who take on the role of customers' eyes and ears in the organisation—coaching, advocating, and supporting enhancements to ensure service is aligned to the customers' perspective of the pivotal customer event.

Leaders' behaviour is also essential to demonstrate the change and signal commitment for the long term. Additionally, explicitly communicating an episode promise to the customer can send a powerful message internally about commitment to changing and improving the customer experience.

Getting better at meeting fundamental customer needs is an imperative for value creation. Engineering the pivotal customer events aligns these efforts and keeps the focus on what really matters to the customer (see sidebar: Improving the Moves Event in Telecommunications).

FOCUS, ALIGNMENT, AND OUTCOMES

As we've seen in this chapter, a strong case can be made for transforming the customer experience around pivotal customer events to create customer value. This is hardly surprising, since these events are a framework that brings a laser-like focus to improving methods to meet customer needs.

The future belongs to organisations that can move beyond the rhetoric of customer centricity, are able to relate to customers on their own terms, and can respond with services that truly meet customers' individual and collective needs. Outstanding customer experiences will be one result, but more importantly, reliable and continuous creation of customer value will be a crucial and lasting source of strategic advantage.

THE LIVEFLOW METHODOLOGY AND ITS BENEFITS

The LiveFlow methodology assembles representatives from all end-to-end activities in one physical location for six to eight weeks and charges them with implementing the high-level design of pivotal customer events, furthering the diagnostic, identifying root causes of customer dissatisfaction, and testing solutions.

LiveFlow focuses on live orders and thus does not disrupt the workflow, allowing the organisation to build solutions that will stand up to the test of reality and garner frontline endorsement.

LiveFlow has delivered outstanding results in more than 20 cases where we have applied it in high-value, high-volume environments. For example, LiveFlow helped reduce processing cycle time at a consumer credit card company by 75 per cent, slashed installation cycle time by 80 per cent at a managed data network provider, and shortened processing cycle time by more than 80 per cent at a consumer mortgage provider.

IMPROVING THE MOVES EVENT IN TELECOMMUNICATIONS

Until recently, only about 40 per cent of a telecoms provider's customers were moved on time—that is, on the right day and with no lapse in service. Botched moves were affecting 300,000 residential and 40,000 small business customers annually, resulting in increased costs and complexity associated with errors and rework. Customers gave the move experience a net promoter score of -46, and complaints were reaching the executive team on a weekly basis.

Focusing on the end-to-end moves event, the telecoms provider redesigned the process to improve the end-to-end customer experience and operations—and in less than six months, it achieved a step change in customer and staff experience.

ADVOCOCY AND SHAREHOLDER IMPACT ON MOVES EVENT

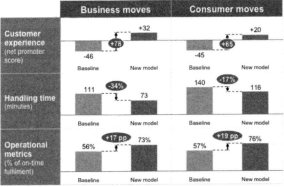

Source: A.T. Kearney

CHAPTER 7

EMBRACE PRODUCTIVITY
AS A STRATEGIC CAPABILITY

As we saw in our opening chapter, Australia has been on a journey of increasing national prosperity for the past 20 years. We have witnessed a dramatic increase in income—the result of judicious and fortunate choices in political, economic, social, and commercial spheres. Even discounting for inflation, GDP has risen 85 per cent since 1994, and GDP per capita has become the highest of any G20 nation.[63]

Australia's growth has been mostly driven by better productivity and improving terms of trade. In the 1990s, before the resource boom, productivity improvements accounted for more than 95 per cent of Australia's income growth. A decade later, the contribution from productivity improvement has dropped to 50 per cent, with improved terms of trade representing 35 per cent of the growth.[64] However, in recent times as the resource boom has slowed, our terms of trade have declined.[65]

Australia's demographics have also complicated this situation. As described in our first chapter, our population is ageing, which means that the proportion of working population will decline, and costs such as aged care and pensions will rise.[66]

To maintain our lifestyle and afford rising demographic costs, Australia needs to reignite its productivity engine; otherwise, we face the prospect of declining relative income, living standards, and national prosperity. Furthermore, achieving productivity is essential to create the headroom for innovation and investments that many, if not all, of the capabilities that are needed for the next 20 years will demand.

Fortunately, the need to improve productivity is now well understood. It has been a topic of public debate for years, with both public and private institutions offering recommendations. Much of this commentary, however, has been at the macro level—specifically, how can the government influence Australia's productivity?

In this chapter, we do not aim to build on the macroeconomic discussion; rather, we introduce a framework that goes beyond the boardroom discussions at individual companies and seeks to raise the bar of what it means for an organisation to embrace productivity as a strategic capability.

Just as companies recognise the need to build organisation-wide capabilities to deliver customer value or become more agile, they need to build the capability to think of productivity more strategically. Productivity cannot simply be a euphemism for cost reduction.

To succeed during the next 20 years, Australian companies need to build true productivity over time. For productivity to be a true strategic capability, it needs to be developed over three horizons: close the gap, maintain the lead, and change the game. Most companies are still only focusing on the first.

To build productivity as a strategic capability is to establish the ability and the culture to boost productivity sustainably by focusing more on increasing the value being created than on reducing the cost base. In doing so, we come one step closer to creating an Australia that is Luckier by Design. The rather unsatisfactory alternative is to sawtooth between being productive and unproductive through sporadic cost-cutting programs.

A DECADE OF DECLINING PRODUCTIVITY GROWTH

Australia's productivity, as measured using multifactor productivity (MFP), has been increasing modestly at an annual average rate of 0.3 per cent over the past 20 years, thanks to improvements in technology, business practices, and regulation. However, productivity has declined by 0.7 per cent per year over the past decade (see figure 28).[67]

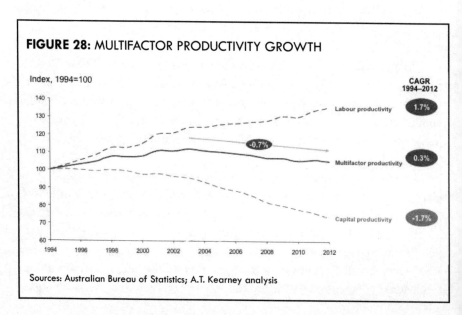

FIGURE 28: MULTIFACTOR PRODUCTIVITY GROWTH

Index, 1994=100

CAGR
1994–2012

Labour productivity — 1.7%

-0.7%

Multifactor productivity — 0.3%

Capital productivity — -1.7%

Sources: Australian Bureau of Statistics; A.T. Kearney analysis

This slow decline between 2002 and 2012 has been driven by falling capital productivity, despite increasing labour productivity. What exactly is happening?

Enormous capital has been injected into the mining sector over the past 10 or 15 years. These investments have delivered aggressive income growth, but they have not increased productivity. Three factors explain this phenomenon:

- **Output lag.** Investments in the resource sector involve large-scale projects that take many years to start generating benefits.

- **Diminishing returns.** The yield of resource projects tends to decline as resources become more expensive to extract.

- **Abundance effect.** When capital is abundant, the level of scrutiny on investments tends to relax and suboptimal projects are approved. Additionally, labour productivity loses focus, and growth becomes a higher priority than workforce output improvement.

At the same time, however, sectors such as agriculture and, to a lesser extent finance, construction, and retail, have increased productivity (see figure 29).

Multifactor productivity in agriculture has risen by 3 per cent a year since 1994. Farmers have become more efficient because of external pressures such as a declining labour force (as farmworkers leave for cities or other industries), international competition, and deteriorating terms of trade. Farms have consolidated and invested in capital equipment, further increasing the output per worker.

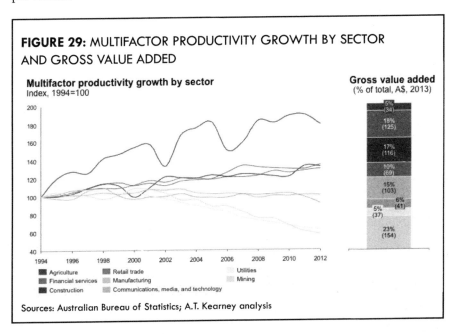

FIGURE 29: MULTIFACTOR PRODUCTIVITY GROWTH BY SECTOR AND GROSS VALUE ADDED

Sources: Australian Bureau of Statistics; A.T. Kearney analysis

Similarly, the financial services industry has experienced a sustained 2 per cent average annual increase in multifactor productivity since 1994, primarily the result of improved labour productivity, technological advancement, and better risk management. However, the contribution of agriculture and financial services to Australia's overall gross value added is 23 per cent—not enough to offset the effect of mining and utilities, which constitute 28 per cent of the value added.

Comparing Australia to other OECD members further highlights the need to refocus on productivity. As economist Saul Eslake found in 2011, overall productivity growth in Australia has slowed more than in many other OECD countries.[68] Australia fell from the 11th fastest-growing nation in the 1990s to the 25th in the following decade. Even in terms of labour productivity, Australia dropped from 11th to 17th. In 1998, our labour productivity was 91.6 per cent that of the United States. Fast forward to 2010, and we have dropped to 84.2 per cent—the lowest level since 1973. This means an American worker is nearly 19 per cent more productive than an Australian worker for an equivalent job.

REDISCOVERING THE NUMERATOR IN THE PRODUCTIVITY EQUATION

Productivity has come to be used as shorthand for cost cutting. Figure 30 shows the number of times productivity is mentioned in annual reports of ASX40 companies. The good news is that the high number of instances (22 times in the mining sector) demonstrates that productivity improvement is at the top of the Australian business community's mind.

However, a review of the next level of articulation of the productivity agenda reveals a slightly different story. Statements such as "controlling costs and improving productivity" and "lowering the cost base and improving productivity" illustrate that reducing cost remains the key focus of productivity initiatives across companies in Australia.

Clearly, reducing input costs is important, and cost-cutting programs can drive short-term improvements. They are, however, difficult to sustain because of the lack of a fundamental transformation in the way of doing things. The unfortunate reality is that the typical cost-cutting approach tends to fall short of truly solving the productivity conundrum.

We believe true productivity requires a focus on both the numerator (output) and the denominator (input) to create sustainable value.

THINKING OF PRODUCTIVITY AS A STRATEGIC CAPABILITY

To raise productivity to the level of a strategic capability, organisations will need

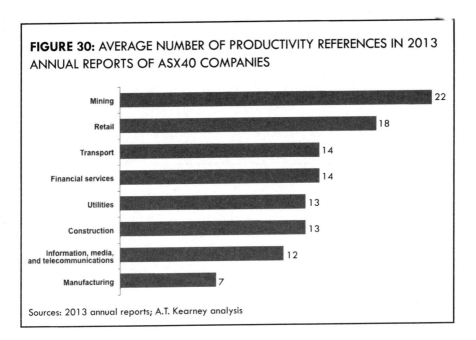

FIGURE 30: AVERAGE NUMBER OF PRODUCTIVITY REFERENCES IN 2013 ANNUAL REPORTS OF ASX40 COMPANIES

Sources: 2013 annual reports; A.T. Kearney analysis

to close the gap, maintain the lead, and change the game. A simple way to visualise these three horizons is by using the productivity capability staircase—illustrated in this example with the Cobb-Douglas production framework, which represents the empirical relationship between output and the combination of factors or inputs used to obtain it (see figure 31).

To improve productivity consistently over time—from both a cost and a value perspective—stop thinking of productivity as a program and start thinking of it as a capability. Companies need to inject productivity into how they do business. Very few Australian firms have reached this stage of maturity. We believe this needs to change: Australian companies will have to make progress up this staircase over the next 20 years.

CLOSE THE GAP

Closing the gap takes an organisation to the theoretical optimum level of productivity that it can currently reach. It is reducing waste and inefficiency—and hence focused primarily on optimising inputs, while closing any gaps with peers in terms of outputs. Closing the gap may involve improving beyond industry standards but normally focuses on one or two dimensions only.

Several tools or methodologies are used to drive productivity at this stage: Six Sigma, systems thinking, lean, and business process engineering, to name

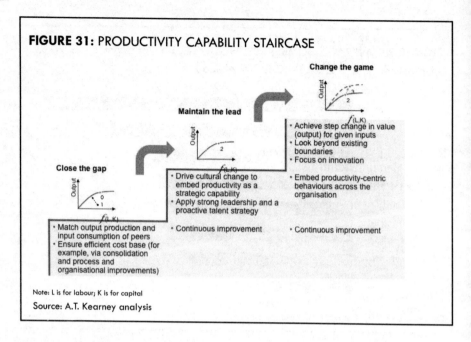

FIGURE 31: PRODUCTIVITY CAPABILITY STAIRCASE

Note: L is for labour; K is for capital

Source: A.T. Kearney analysis

just a few. The list can be confusing. In essence, these tools are approaches to pull one or more of three core efficiency levers:

Organisation enhancement and realignment. Look for opportunities to develop a leaner, simpler, and more cost-effective structure. Productivity improvements traditionally come from combining roles, realigning spans of control, and reducing hierarchical layers. The by-product of such enhancements is an organisation that moves close to achieving the DNA to be agile, as outlined in chapters four and five.

Physical consolidation. Evaluate centralisation and offshoring or outsourcing opportunities for scalable activities and operations, such as back-office processing or distribution centres. In large companies with a long history of mergers and acquisitions, this lever tends to be one of the most relevant, as integrations at first are often only partial, often intentionally so to mitigate the level of organisational disruption and risk.

Process improvement. Examine the key processes in the value chain, and identify opportunities to eliminate non-value-adding activities (especially when viewed from the customer's perspective), reduce any instances of unvalued over-service, and decrease manual work or rework through increased automation and standardisation.

Closing the gap is the easiest step. Maintaining the change is where most organisations start to struggle. Companies often manage to identify their main productivity gaps and launch improvement initiatives but may only reap the benefits for a short time because performance starts to backslide. They get caught in a sawtooth pattern where they improve productivity, fall back, then improve again for three to four years but fall back again. And the cycle keeps going.

MAINTAIN THE LEAD

Sustaining productivity improvements is hard and involves two main components: operational and behavioural. The operational component encompasses the actual changes in systems, process flows, policies, and so forth. These are typically adjusted in larger steps as part of the improvement initiatives and tend to be the focus of most productivity improvement programs. In most cases, however, operational changes need to be followed by adjustments to individuals' behaviours. For example, if a new order tracking system is put in place to replace manual paperwork, the productivity benefit is only realised when salespeople actually stop doing the manual paperwork—something they are often reluctant to do. Pursuing these behavioural changes is vital for getting full value from productivity improvement programs. Maintaining the lead requires ongoing optimisation, of both smaller operational changes to adjust systems, process flows, and policies and of behaviour in pursuit of smarter work practices.

For organisations to achieve this level of capability, employees need to believe in and feel accountable for the change—and not see productivity as something being done to them. Four elements go a long way in helping to embed this capability:

- **Make productivity a board priority and agenda item.** Driving deep change requires senior leaders to sponsor change—to talk about it constantly (and constructively) and set the example of new behaviours expected from the rest of the organisation.
- **Nurture productivity-savvy talent.** Behavioural change will often demand new skills and capabilities from existing employees. To maintain the change, therefore, they need training and development programs that set them up for success in the new way of doing things. Frequently, attracting and letting go of specific talent is also required to maintain behavioural change. Companies often underinvest in capability building when it comes to productivity—a critical oversight that often leads to the sawtooth effect.
- **Measure and manage for the right performance.** Ensure that a few clear, quantifiable, and easy-to-understand metrics are defined to monitor changes in performance. Tracking is important, but perhaps more important is the ability to create a tight feedback loop and the ability to drill

down to diagnose efficiently any slippage in near-real time. If we focus on results as key metrics rather than the more comfortable and common focus on progress on productivity initiatives or hitting a budget, we can create a real sense of ownership and accountability towards the ends rather than an obsession with the means.

- **Make continuous improvement the norm.** A continuous improvement mindset needs to be cultivated across the organisation for it to be seen as achieving this productivity capability level. Setting up a dedicated continuous improvement function or role is a good step, but ultimately, with or without a continuous improvement team, functions need to be accountable for driving their own journey.

Consider the example of a formerly state-owned British enterprise with nearly £10 billion turnover. A culture and capability turnaround enabled it to maintain its productivity lead. Many improvement programs had been conducted over the years, but each time, performance slipped back to where it had begun. The company needed to maintain performance—not just to remain profitable, but to expand with increasing volumes to meet customer requirements.

The company ran a four-stage transformation program to improve the efficiency and effectiveness of its shared services:

Stage 1: Initiation took a Six Sigma approach to process improvement, introduced 5S principles to establish foundations for continuous improvement, standardised processes and obtained ISO accreditation, and raised capabilities through training and hiring new talent.

Stage 2: Growth gradually centralised resources, strengthened continuous improvement practices, and shifted ownership to internal specialists (rather than third-party coaches). Internal personnel were involved in developing the vision to instil ownership and control over the transformation.

Stage 3: Maturity broadened ownership of continuous improvement from specialists to everyone, trained all leaders on continuous improvement to arm them with the required skills, maintained close alignment with key program stakeholders, and nurtured collaboration and cross-pollination among teams.

Stage 4: Business as usual inculcated continuous improvement as the normal way of working.

Ten years after the start of the program, the enterprise sustains these transformation benefits and operates at a fundamentally different productivity level. The program has more than halved costs, enabled consolidation of locations, brought attrition and absence under control, and more than doubled employee productivity.

CHANGE THE GAME

The third and final level in turning productivity into a strategic capability involves changing the game. Organisations that reach this stage tend to follow three rules:

FOCUS ON PRODUCTIVITY OVER MULTIPLE YEARS ON MULTIPLE FRONTS

To illustrate what a multiyear, multifront focus looks like, let's examine financial services.

Australian retail banks have been globally recognised for their remarkable performance over the past decade. These businesses have taken their productivity capability to the next level through two pillars: technology and customer centricity.

Technology. In contrast to many other developed countries, banks such as Commonwealth Bank of Australia and National Australia Bank have been steadily replacing core banking systems. This has made activities cheaper, faster, and more accurate for the banks and for customers. With the arrival of the mobile era, banks are further driving productivity improvements by self-enabling customers across channels, being more analytical and insightful, and automating supply chains.

Customer centricity. A focus on the customer is also driving productivity and increased customer satisfaction at all Australian retail banks. Initiatives have taken place or are underway at several financial institutions to shift the focus to the customer by retraining or replacing the traditional branch staff mindset with a friendlier customer service approach that borrows heavily from other retail industries. What is more convenient and less hassle for the customer is often also more efficient for the bank.

FIND VALUE BEYOND EXISTING ORGANISATIONAL BOUNDARIES

There is no doubt that organisations can constantly reinvent themselves and evolve, generating both incremental and step-change improvements. There is, however, a limit to how much they can improve within their four walls. To reach new levels of productivity, a company needs to look beyond its own confines and examine the productivity of the entire supply and distribution network (similar to the themes explored in the chapter Unlock Shared Value). Identifying and developing strategic partnerships with key suppliers allows organisations to unlock the next level of strategic value captured across four dimensions:[69]

- **Value chain optimisation.** Close collaboration with suppliers allows for reduced inventory levels and improved forecasting.

- **Structural capabilities.** Suppliers can provide a sustainable cost advantage or increased flexibility, responsiveness, and scalability.
- **Risk management.** Suppliers can collaborate on turning potential operational risks into opportunities to gain advantage.
- **Growth.** Suppliers have differentiating capabilities such as innovation (R&D) or broader geographic reach that can enable growth.

Australian supermarkets are already breaking through their four walls to create value beyond their boundaries. One leading player has undertaken a large-scale supply chain optimisation program, addressing inefficiencies in multiple areas (such as sourcing, inventory management, and distribution) through close collaboration with its suppliers. In addition, this grocer's expansion into financial services and the creation of long-term contracts directly with farmers has generated value beyond its four walls.

Another leading supermarket has reaped productivity benefits from expanding into adjacent categories, acquiring a shopper insights third party, and focusing on the productivity of fruit and vegetable suppliers via grants focused on efficient water use, managing nutrients, and reducing their carbon footprint.

The leading grocery players have worked with suppliers to minimise product handling from the production line to the shelves with initiatives such as shelf-ready packaging—that is, boxes and crates suitable to be directly displayed to shoppers.

Companies in Australia are already driving integrated supply chain collaboration initiatives, and based on what we have seen in other markets, we expect this trend to intensify in the next 10 years.

INNOVATE FOR PRODUCTIVITY

Innovation drives productivity, primarily through two avenues. First, it improves the products and processes that keep a business running. Improved products lead to increased demand and with it a potential to capitalise on benefits such as economies of scale, greater labour and capital utilisation, and job specialisation. Innovation in processes also lifts productivity by designing more efficient ways to produce and deliver products and services. Second, innovation in a particular firm creates pressure on incumbents and new entrants to squeeze out their own inefficiencies to compete. This combined effect raises the productivity of the whole system.

There is a strong, positive relationship between the innovation activity of a firm and its productivity level and growth.[70] In Australia, research by the Department of Innovation suggests that businesses that innovate are more than twice as likely to report increased output per hour worked.[71] This evidence confirms the importance of integrating innovation as part of a game-changing strategic productivity capability. Furthermore, the next 20 years will present unique challenges and opportunities requiring disruptive thinking. Thus, the ability to anticipate the broad contours of likely disruption, and to innovate to unlock productivity opportunities, will become a hallmark of stage three productivity.

In Australia, however, innovation has not had the same level of focus as in other countries. Our R&D spend is 2.1 per cent of GDP, which is below that of countries such as the United States (3 per cent) or Finland (4 per cent).[72] Data at the individual firm level also confirms the gap. In the United Kingdom, for example, companies spend between 20 and 40 per cent more on innovation than we do. Moreover, when Australian businesses innovate they tend to focus on product innovation (new and exciting things to sell) rather than process innovation (new and exciting ways to build and deliver products).[73] For Australian businesses to thrive in the next 20 years, these trends need to be challenged, and innovation must become second nature for our companies. We are smaller than our global counterparts, which means we should naturally be more nimble—both domestically and regionally.

LIFTING PRODUCTIVITY TO A STRATEGIC CAPABILITY

Companies can start to lift productivity into a strategic capability by honestly assessing where they sit on the productivity capability staircase. Many may find themselves at stage one.

The next step is to reach a consensus that stage two is worth pursuing; agreeing on that principle is essential before organisations venture into building stage two capabilities. This is harder than it sounds. Real trade-offs will need to be made in terms of where leaders focus and how performance is measured. Stage two is where productivity turns from something that takes the form of a program to something that feels like a capability.

For those that do achieve stage two, the choice to move to stage three presents itself. For a daring few, stages two and three may be attempted in parallel. Whatever the choice, the journey over the next 20 years is going to be a long one as Australian businesses go beyond cost cutting and nurture productivity back into the organisation as a truly strategic capability.

CHAPTER 8

GAIN ADVANTAGE THROUGH ANALYTICS

D uring the next 20 years, analytics will become more important, but it is about far more than data—big or otherwise. It is about building a pervasive analytics culture with a clear vision, strong capability, and C-suite support to leverage data-enabled insights that fundamentally improve the competitive position of firms in Australia and around the world.

Companies will realise the full benefits of analytics with ongoing investment in the discipline, embedding it in their DNA, and improving the velocity of data-driven insight throughout their organisations. This is not a static proposition. There will be iterations and improvements as technology is adapted and enhanced to drive new insights, automate business routines, enhance customer value propositions, and support more granular optimisation of business decisions in the dynamic economic environment.

LEAD THROUGH ANALYTICS

What is the value of data, big or otherwise? Unless it can be transformed into information, insight, and action, it is of little value to organisations and people entrusted to lead and make value-accretive decisions. Successful players will have the capability to create and capture real value from the data they already have, rather than simply generating more big data. By first drawing and acting on insights from available data, they can build the analytical muscle to extract much greater value from subsequent technology-heavy investments.

All of the aforementioned strategies involving an expansive mindset, agility, pivotal customer events, and productivity rely on information and insight to be effective.

Analytics leads to relevant insights that can be applied to strategies that help organisations create and extract value. Applying analytics falls into many areas. Two opportunities are especially powerful:

DRIVING EFFICIENCY AND EFFECTIVENESS IMPROVEMENTS ALONG THE ENTIRE VALUE CHAIN

Analytics can help improve the value chain. It provides detailed information on customer needs to salespeople, for example, bolstering customised cross-sell and upsell offers and scripts. It can optimise supply levels, distribution, and logistics with granular demand mapping and forecasting. It also can optimise production processes with more sophisticated assessments of bottlenecks and waste, or product design, leading to smarter investment in product elements that are most valued by customers while reducing cost and delivery for those elements that customers do not value as much. Analytics will extend to improvements in outsourcing and offshoring as well. It will provide insights into activities that can be better contracted from functional specialists or other scale-based players in R&D, manufacturing, assessing customer credit histories, or managing customer contact centres. A well-developed analytics capability is crucial for capturing the less obvious, harder to reach gains.

ENHANCING THE CUSTOMER EXPERIENCE AND VALUE PROPOSITIONS

Improving the customer experience and value proposition covers a wide range of opportunities. Analytics, for example, can help airlines proactively provide customers with timely rerouting information for delayed flights or help banks give customers budgeting information based on observations of what thousands of other similar households are spending. For farmers, analytics can develop predictive models using agronomic data and prescribe crop-protection solutions based on weather patterns and their impact on insect populations.

Pursuing these opportunities requires investing not only in technology, but also in the human capital that will be needed to bridge organisational silos and unlock the value embedded in data, which promises to grow exponentially in the coming decades. Creating world-class analytics capabilities will be challenging and will take time to achieve, but it will provide the basis for competitive advantage during the next 20 years.

To lead through analytics, actions to build this capability will need to be overt and pronounced, with the pendulum swinging firmly into the analytics camp in order to grow talent and help skills to flourish. Reaching these goals will require a holistic, transformative approach.

CAPTURING ANALYTICAL VALUE

The rise of the Internet and concurrent investment in IT infrastructure has

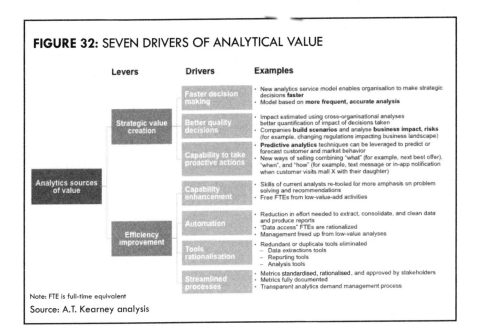

FIGURE 32: SEVEN DRIVERS OF ANALYTICAL VALUE

Note: FTE is full-time equivalent
Source: A.T. Kearney analysis

made data available like never before. The technology to help analyse this data and communicate insight is becoming more sophisticated and affordable, not just for large companies but also for more nimble small and medium enterprises.

So it is not surprising that 67 per cent of business leaders see analytics as a core enabler of business strategy for the coming decade and beyond.[74] We see seven drivers of analytical value, touching both strategic value creation and efficiency improvements, ranging from faster decision making to streamlined processes (see figure 32).[75]

What's more, we anticipate that, in addition to using data and analytics for their own business purposes, more companies will sell this information to complementary businesses for their own development. For example, a telecommunications company may sell its mobile usage data to a retailer, which can use it to identify emerging high-traffic areas of affluent consumers and to target relevant promotions or establish a new store location.

As we scan other industries and functions, it is clear that we have a long way to go before analytics capabilities become ubiquitous (see figure 33). The communications, media, and technology industries and the consumer products and retail industry are early adopters, while automotive is not.

Clear examples of industry developments are appearing. In May 2013, Woolworths announced its acquisition of a 50 per cent share of Quantium, a data analytics company. In July 2013, the chief financial officer of Wesfarmers Limited, Terry Bowen, told *The Australian* that the retail conglomerate was keen to work more closely with its suppliers on using data analytics to target customers more closely and make more efficient use of inventory. Bowen said Wesfarmers remained on the lookout for potential acquisitions of data mining and other e-commerce businesses.

From a functional perspective, the sales and marketing and strategy functions are relatively mature in their analytical capability, while procurement and human resources are playing catch-up.[76] Overall, our research indicates that 10 per cent of firms are considered leaders, with the bulk following, playing catch-up, lagging, or simply waiting. There is clearly an opportunity to develop analytical capabilities.

A 2013 paper in the *International Journal of Research in Marketing* quantified the benefit of an effective marketing analytics department.[77] "Most firms can expect favourable performance outcomes from deploying marketing analytics," the authors said. "Moreover, these favourable performance outcomes should be even greater in industries in which competition is high and in which customers change their needs and wants frequently". In fact, the paper's research highlights that a one-unit increase in the degree of deployment (moving a firm at the median or the 50th percentile of deployment to the 65th percentile) on a scale one to seven is associated with an 8 per cent increase in return on assets.

THE ROLE OF ANALYTICS

However, there is a gap between collecting data and using it to realise its value fully. Even as companies invest millions of dollars to build the capability to capture, manage, analyse, and communicate data, it remains raw information. For businesses to survive and thrive during the next 20 years, analytics will need to be embedded in business practices. Analytics plays an integral role across the business in marketing and sales, operations, and more generally in management decision making. For example, pivotal customer events, productivity, and agility all rely on superior information and insight to be effectively designed and implemented.

Pivotal customer events. This begins with design based on richer customer segment analysis, touch point analysis, and friction analysis. The pivotal customer event is the cornerstone of developing a basis of differentiation and innovation in the customer experience. At its heart is reaching the right insights and understanding sources of customer goals and irritations.

Customers are becoming more demanding and want to be treated as individuals. Through the use of analytics, market leaders have been able to develop a portrait of each customer. They not only know how old their customers are

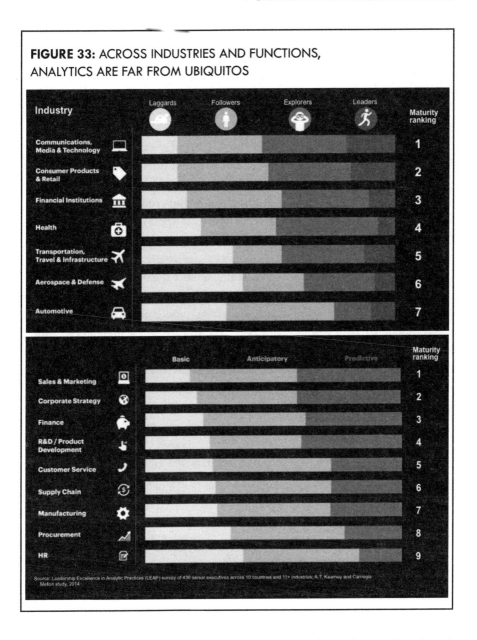

FIGURE 33: ACROSS INDUSTRIES AND FUNCTIONS, ANALYTICS ARE FAR FROM UBIQUITOS

and where they live, but also what their customers say about them to friends and what lifestyle changes they face.

Ford Motor Company, for instance, is learning what their customers may want in future electric vehicles.[78] Current owners of the company's hybrid cars can opt to send data about their use to Ford via an embedded modem in each car. Every time they plug their car in, Ford learns where the owner is, how many gas versus electric miles they drive, and how often they drive. The data is helping Ford plan future hybrid products. "If we know how people are using their vehicle and what they're saying about it [on social media], we can then look at how it relates to our internal business processes," said Mike Cavaretta, Ford's project leader for predictive analytics.

It is not difficult to appreciate the quality of insight that can be drawn from this information. Across the world, organisations are becoming savvier about how they interact with their customers. The first step is, of course, to develop a consistent view of the customer across the organisation. Beyond that, companies can look to anything from social media to machine-to-machine interactions for insight. The understanding some businesses have of their customers is already far-reaching and providing good marketing value. Using historical buying data based on women who have signed up for its baby registries, retailer Target has famously been able to predict which customers are pregnant, the top products they buy when they're expecting, and their due dates, enabling the company to send coupons timed for the right stage of pregnancy.[79] There is, however, also the danger in the growing world of analytics of correlation for correlation's sake. Our examples above demonstrate that it is no longer enough to merely improve one's targeting of potential customers. Leading players will find ways to enhance customer offers and experiences through analytical information and insight. For example, the airline that provides customers with timely rerouting information after flights are delayed could notify hotels and other awaiting services so the domino effect of delays is resolved for what would otherwise be a brand-detracting customer event, as so often happens. Ultimately, analytics will be directive; it will need to be part of a larger purpose to be an effective enabler. By targeting pivotal customer events, organisations can ensure they enact on the critical points of pain, improve customer experience, and therefore secure loyalty.

Productivity. Embracing productivity as a strategic capability requires organisations to tackle productivity on multiple fronts on an ongoing basis. Developing this capability is hard and is yet to be taken on by many Australian companies. There are many dimensions to the task. At the core is optimisation—doing more with less. When we think about sustainable productivity programs, business process reengineering, lean, and Six Sigma come to mind. Common to all these techniques—and the successful programs they underpin—is data and analytics. Yet when organisations embark on these programs, they find their data to be severely lacking and invariably find themselves investing in the analytical tools and capabilities needed to support productivity programs. The capability lags behind the need and, as a result, the opportunity invariably is lost as the undertaking becomes something that is too difficult to execute. It stands to reason that an analytically capable organisation will be better placed to leverage the tools to drive productivity.

A more advanced analytical capability will help this productivity drive through optimisation of resources, both human and capital. For example, looking at supply chain productivity, we see that much more value can be unlocked by using optimisation techniques. Consider a recent case involving the procurement of logistics services for a consumer goods company. The typical negotiation with suppliers would yield a 3 per cent price reduction. However, after undertaking network optimisation to improve the selection of the supplier to use on particular routes, the price negotiation yielded more than a 6 per cent cost reduction. Taking this one step further with a collaborative optimisation approach, which simultaneously considers current supply market conditions, preferred network configuration and individual company capabilities unlocked more than 10 per cent in value.

The data and tools for collaborative optimisation exist today, but the expertise to undertake these sorts of exercises largely sits outside organisations. Furthermore, traditionally, optimisation has been a point-in-time exercise, whereas by 2034, we expect this to be dynamic, readily available, and repeatable. A current example of this is dynamic decision making (DDM), which optimises supply arrangements, often existing ones, on a frequent basis, often weekly, which is unlocking 1 to 3 per cent of value. DDM and other evolving techniques are identifying undiscovered productivity benefits through the use of analytic capability.

Agility. Being agile begins with our definition of agility: the capability and cultural mindset that enables an organisation to lead in dynamic conditions and implement change as a matter of routine towards a distinct purpose. The benefits of this are articulated in chapter five: Be Agile. As with pivotal customer events and productivity, analytics will be a key enabler of agility. An organisation with a strong analytics capability will be able to provide information and insight to support superior decision-making ability, such as data mining of social media feeds, which lets organisations quickly identify emerging trends. However, only agile organisations with analytical capability will be able to capitalise on the insights. Predictive and scenario analytics will also help anticipate opportunities, risks, and options for addressing them.

Central to achieving this agility is the integration of acumen in three areas—business, analytics, and IT systems—to form the analytics trilingual, equally conversant in three languages:

- **The language of business** to understand profit and loss statements, strategy, marketing, and all relevant business issues: Business acumen deals with how and where the rubber hits the road in terms of executing ideas driven from analytics—what can and cannot be deployed in a real business environment.

- **The language of analytics** to understand what is possible by crossing variables X and Y, which is the ability to conceptualise ways for gaining the insights that would materially affect an organisation's understanding of their business: This is the language to use with statisticians and modellers to translate highly complex analyses into easy-to-understand elements for business users.

- **The language of IT** for an understanding of the universe of live systems, which help run the business and identify where the data is and how it can be made available so relevant insights can be generated: Systems and IT acumen also helps shape the future design of the capture and management of rapidly escalating data, collect the most essential information, and provide it to the organisation in a timely fashion, allowing it to be used effectively.

Integrating these three types of acumen is crucial for asking the right kinds of questions. In fact, the kinds of analyses and systems needed are often very simple; the missing ingredient is asking the right question to find the key insights.

As organisations develop the human and technical analytic capabilities, the processes to provide insight and drive decisions will be delivered in a more efficient and dynamic manner, far more so than today. In combination, these factors will improve organisational fitness and agility.

BUILDING ANALYTICS CAPABILITY

Analytics brings together many competencies—some that may exist and others that will need to be developed, some that will be held by specialist resources while others will be embedded in the broader organisation. Beyond this, analytics is a way of working, a part of the culture and fabric of the organisation. Those that succeed and reap the rewards will see this as a journey that will fuel their growth.

Making analytics part of the organisational DNA is achieved by investing in the analytical capability and ensuring that the overall corporate strategy provides a clear direction so analytics is considered a core competency. As is the case with acquiring other new capabilities, actions for attaining advanced analytics will need to be overt and pronounced to grow talent and help skills flourish. A holistic, and even transformative, approach helps companies reach their goals. There are four areas to address to become a world-class analytics organisation (see figure 34).

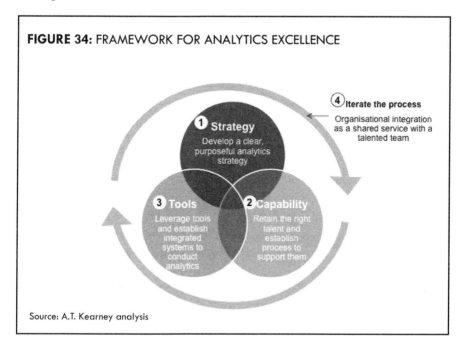

FIGURE 34: FRAMEWORK FOR ANALYTICS EXCELLENCE

Source: A.T. Kearney analysis

STRATEGY: ANTICIPATE THE ANALYSIS WITH A CLEAR, PURPOSEFUL ANALYTICS STRATEGY

Formulating a vision for analytics involves outlining the scope and ambition for the capability, ensuring it supports the strategic direction of the organisation across the value chain and all functional areas and addresses the policies regarding the people, processes, and technology for achieving the vision. At its core, it requires organisations to move from opinion to evidence-based decision making. Thus, a significant hurdle many organisations face in formulating their analytics strategy is in determining how analytical insights will add value to the different parts of the organisation. This can be particularly hard if staff have not seen analytics as the key decision driver (and maintain an 'opinion'-based approach).

Working with key stakeholders to identify functional and business objectives for analytics will ensure that there is internal alignment regarding the goals that will be targeted through analytics. Successful, sustainable execution of this strategy will require taking not just a project or even program-based approach, but a transformative approach that will change the way business is done.

CAPABILITY: GENERATE THE INSIGHTS WITH ANALYTICAL CAPABILITIES AND SERVICES

A recent A.T. Kearney study found that only 10 per cent of companies have the analytical competency needed to affect business results strongly and drive competitive advantage. Those that have a more advanced analytical capability are generally in industries where the consumer touch points are more mature.

Developing the analytical capabilities and service involves the integration of IT, data warehousing, business intelligence, combining structured and unstructured data, and leveraging machine-learning algorithms to increasingly replace a statistical model. But beyond the technology addressing the talent and cultural issues is perhaps the biggest challenge organisations face in building their analytics capability. Analysts will close the gap by asking the right questions focused on business value. Finding and integrating analysts with the right skill and capabilities within the Australian market, which is short of talent, means rethinking the people and culture function to ensure that its actions, and those of the organisation, support growing the analytics capability.

Organisations will walk before they run. A staged approach, so the organisation can see the value before going further, is vital to get the analytics transformation off the ground.

The type of capability to which we are referring cannot be transplanted into an organisation without the support, training, career pathways, and engagements that will allow analytical talent to thrive. For example, procurement functions in many organisations are actively strengthening their analytics capabilities to understand history more clearly and leverage this knowledge to provide better insights into business opportunities. Unfortunately, the typical approach is to hire analysts and place them in teams that often are not capable of understanding the value or need for the analytical horsepower, because team members lack the understanding to direct and leverage these resources effectively. So the analysts become underused and disenfranchised and often opt out.

In addition to hiring talented analysts, involving top management and encouraging a suitable analytics culture will help a firm realise the benefits of analytics.[80] Just like IT of 20 years ago, which saw the evolution of the IT staffer to the IT manager to the chief information officer, we foresee the creation and advent of the chief data and analytics officer. Historically, data provision and quality of information were mainly viewed from the perspective of risks and costs. However, it is quickly becoming apparent that those who can draw insights from data will outperform in all areas.

TOOLS: IMPLEMENT THE INSIGHTS WITH ANALYTICAL OPERATIONS AND PROCESSES

Once the basics are mastered and the capability is progressing past purely transactional or reactive work, analytics can be embedded in a wider range of management processes to influence a wider range of business decisions directly. They include knowledge management, defining and monitoring service levels and compliance, evaluating performance, and optimising business responses.

An organisation with a mature analytics capability will have integrated systems with sophisticated workflow—a global source of truth that feeds directly into business decisions.

Increasingly, the world will move towards more real-time analytics, trigger-based marketing, servicing, risk assessment, and other related techniques. The challenge here is that a lot of the artificial intelligence, particularly the current generation, is rules-based and not cognitive or self-learning. This difference clearly poses the risk that without oversight, particularly from the trilingual perspective, what should be insights will rapidly become system errors.

There is also the real risk that organisations will lose their agility, rather than enhance it. They will become paralysed by the analysis as they attempt to move from opinion to evidence-based decision making often described as paralysis by analysis. How to solve this will need to be an explicit part of any analytics-capability building-transformation.

REPEAT THE PROCESS: INTEGRATE ACROSS THE ORGANISATION AS A SHARED SERVICE

Approaching analytics as a shared service, similar to other corporate functions such as human resources, IT, or finance, will elevate it to a critical core competency. As with other corporate functions, the right organisation structure will depend on a range of factors, such as the size and diversity of the business, the need to develop specialist expertise, and a culture of collaboration across business units. Each approach has its benefits and challenges and will evolve as the size and significance of the capability develops (see figure 35). The objective is to attract leading talent, provide strong career paths, develop specialists who will become known across the organisation, and support the development of cutting-edge practices that can be cascaded across the organisation.

THE 20-YEAR HORIZON

Recent research has shown that Moore's law is faltering. As chip technology reaches atomic levels, manufacturing limits and the inflection point for the size-cost rela-

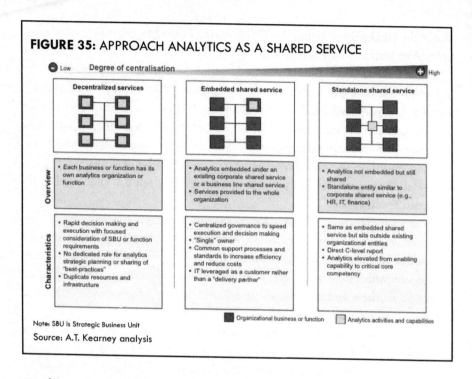

FIGURE 35: APPROACH ANALYTICS AS A SHARED SERVICE

Note: SBU is Strategic Business Unit

Source: A.T. Kearney analysis

tionship are reached. However, the discipline of artificial intelligence continues to grow, as does connectivity and the size of global networks. We don't see technology being the barrier to analytics capability, but rather, the use and application of the technology, embedded in the organisation, becomes the key obstacle to overcome.

Just as the enterprise resource planning system was a competitive advantage in the 20th century, analytics has the potential to provide an edge in the 21st century. The difference is that it won't be an IT platform that provides the basis for competitive advantage. Instead, it will be human capital with the ability to synthesise information from multiple sources to influence business decisions that will set companies apart. Analytical tools will play the support role dependent upon the right application environment in the hands of experienced practitioners. The Melbourne Business School is now offering a master's degree program in business analytics. The demand for trilingual speakers and analytically-capable staff members, who are literate in mathematics and strategy and knowledgeable about IT systems, is growing and is likely to remain ahead of supply. This mismatch could be the bottleneck to rapid deployment and building of the analytics capability across all sectors.

The future will not be single analytical projects; rather, it will be a seamless integration of data and analytics throughout organisations in order to solve business problems. Rather than focusing on a single, big data set, organisations will begin to master the challenges of housing different parts of data in multiple databases and technology platforms. We will be looking for more sophisticated and nimble solutions to extract data effectively and create a single source of insight.

But while data is a crucial element of success, it will not be the only element.[81] While some analysis will become automated, based on algorithms to determine next logical product or targeting, algorithms for churn propensity modelling, and those suggesting preferred scripts, other analysis will involve analysts making pragmatic decisions regarding the problems they are trying to solve and the data required. Otherwise, there is a risk of getting lost in the data and missing the value and insight that could result.

Achieving functional excellence takes time to develop and mature. As with all new capabilities, actions will need to be overt, with the pendulum swinging firmly into the analytical camp if they are to be given the chance to grow and flourish. This was the case with IT 20 years ago when we saw the evolution from the IT helper into the IT manager and later into the chief information officer, we similarly foresee the creation and advent of the chief data officer and chief analytics officer to drive the development of more sophisticated analytics capabilities. Successful companies will tackle this development methodically and comprehensively, starting with the capability to create and capture real value from the data already available within the organisation, not just generate more big-data for some possible future use. Developing an analytics capability will not be easy or quick and thus will provide a basis of competitive advantage over the coming 20 years. So being purposeful and starting now is an imperative for those companies wanting to remain relevant and succeed in the longer term.

PART V: PREPARING FOR TOMORROW'S CHALLENGES

L ooking back on our economic history, Australia has demonstrated its resilience in the face of challenging circumstances on more than one occasion.

From the boom of the gold rush to the pits of the great depression; from an economy built "on the sheep's back" to the recession we had to have and, more recently, to the mining boom, in each case we have overcome challenges, and ridden waves of prosperity.

A series of economic reforms contributed to a productivity surge in the 1990s, followed by very strong demand for commodities, mainly from Asia, in the 2000s.

Now, after two decades of sustained growth and economic good fortune, we believe Australia and Australian business will be called on again to demonstrate its resilience and strength.

It will be an uncomfortable and challenging time for Australia, one in which old formulas do not lead to predictable results. When traditional capabilities fall short of what is required and deeply-held convictions are challenged.

The future will be inherently uncertain. Rather than try to anticipate it, we believe the strongest and most fitting response for Australian business is to arm itself with the necessary capabilities, those encapsulated in our Capability Manifesto, to navigate this uncertainty towards the opportunities which we believe the double-edged megatrends present.

We believe that Australia, Australian business, and the Australian people have the potential to do so and to thrive—to move from strength to strength. Our strong economic position, the financial robustness of our businesses today, and the determination and pragmatism of our people put us in a privileged position to chart our own destiny—to write the next chapter in our economic history.

The first step is one of introspection by the leaders and the boards of Australian business. How does my company fare today against the Capability Manifesto? Where are we particularly strong? What are our areas of weakness? What will it take to round out our capabilities? And, what is getting in our way today?

As this journey unfolds, we hope this book contributes in some way to shaping the dialogue within Australian business and offers leaders a framework to shape the efforts to prepare their companies for the next two decades of opportunity and challenge. We believe this book represents the start of a dialogue—one which must begin today but will likely unfold over many years to come.

In two decades' time, in 2034, those in power today will have retired and passed leadership to the next generation. Those starting their careers today will be occupying the executive office. The businesses that will lead the ASX may have not even been founded. The concept of a world without the internet and mobile phones will be a distant, and hard to imagine, memory. Today's technology and ideas will seem antiquated and anachronistic. It is towards this future that we launch ourselves, our businesses, and our nation in search of "Australia 2034: Luckier by Design".

Twenty years into our own journey with Australia, we at A.T. Kearney, remain excited by what lies ahead and look forward to playing our part.

ACKNOWLEDGEMENTS

This book is the culmination of ideas, insights, and perspectives of our many A.T. Kearney colleagues—those with whom we work today and those who have left the firm but remain our friends and co-collaborators. The book would not have been possible without a willingness to share the knowledge and wisdom derived from client engagements—with special thanks to Ceyda Atay, Peter Ayre, Aditja Bajaj, Carolyn Bennett, Robert Bustos-McNeil, Carmen Chau, Peter Cook, Noemie Creteur, Peter David, James Deighton, Adam Dixon, Rob Feeney, Kylie Gao, Sid Ghosh, Kate Hart, Ariel Hersh, Terry Innerst, Nawaz Isaji, Yogesh Khadilkar, Robert Kuijken, Clare Latham, Natalie Lee, Sam Lewis, Harman Lidder, Kathryn Londrigan, Maria Martinez, Toni Mladenova, Varun Mohankumar, VT Mukundan, Alyssa Pei, Nick Raper, Enrico Rizzon, Marc Thiebaut, Jonathon Tietke, Daniel Tram, Anna Videira-Johnson, and Suzanne Weston.

We also appreciate the efforts of those who provided valuable and ongoing support throughout the book development process, including Sarovar Aggarwal, Fred Avellen, Madhur Baghat, Jeremy Barker, Alex Butiri, Stuart Butterworth, Patricia Campos, Ani Chakraborty, Elaine Chan, Shyamala Chandrasekar, Caroline Clarke, Amanda DeCook, Linda Deng, Celine Develay, Alison Dunn, Gavin Edgley, Joel Fleischmann, Scott Glover, David Gowans, Geir Haga, Robert Harriss, Peter Huggins, Reginald Jigins, Bronwyn Kitchen, Lorin Knive, Morten Lauritsen, Collin Li, Chris Livitsanis, Adam Maddocks, Ankit Mishra, Kishan Modi, Benoit Nachtergaele, Adam Qaiser, Liselle Regis, Alex Romanov, Matthew Sek, Anshuman Sengar, Elizabeth Scott, Zorawar Singh, Rohen Sood, Narelle Stevens, Jason Taleb, David Tay, Justin Tor, Nathan Tuck, Rhiannon Thomas, Jithan Varma, Frank Wohlfarth, and Ajay Yadav.

Finally, we are grateful to David Woods and Laura Hawkins at LID Publishing for their enthusiastic support and close cooperation.

REFERENCES

[1] All monetary amounts are Australian dollars unless noted as U.S. dollars.

[2] Australian Bureau of Statistics, 5368.0 International Trade in Goods and Services, accessed 9 June 2014; Australian Department of Foreign Affairs and Trade

[3] Australian Bureau of Statistics, 5655.0 Managed Funds, accessed 9 June 2014

[4] Organisation for Economic Co-operation and Development, Income Distribution and Poverty, accessed 9 June 2014

[5] Australian Bureau of Statistics, 45170DO001 Prisoners in Australia, accessed 9 June 2014

[6] Australian Bureau of Statistics; NetActuary; Bruce Tranter and Robert White, "Share-ownership and the triple bottom line: A preliminary study," paper presented at the Australian Sociological Association Conference, Sydney, 2001

[7] Australian Bureau of Statistics; Australian Taxation Office; "A third of Aussies prefer smartphone over TV", Financial Review, 30 July 2013

[8] Australian Bureau of Statistics; Ben Pike, "Vietnamese surname Nguyen to overtake Smith as most common metropolitan surname", news.com.au, 31 May 2013

[9] Interest coverage ratio=EBIT/(Interest expenses)

[10] Australian Bureau of Statistics

[11] Productivity Commission, "Review of National Competition Policy Reforms," report no. 33 (2005)

[12] International Monetary Fund, World Economic Outlook Database, April 2014

[13] Organisation for Economic Co-operation and Development, International Migration Database, accessed 1 September 2014

[14] Australian Government, "Australia in the Asian Century", white paper, October 2012

[15] United Nations, UN Comtrade Database, accessed 16 September 2014. Key Asian economies are China, India, Indonesia, Japan, and South Korea.

[16] Australian Department of Foreign Affairs and Trade; Australian Bureau of Statistics

[17] Organisation for Economic Co-operation and Development, Outflows and Inflows of Foreign Direct Investment, accessed 16 September 2014

[18] "What Do Mature Consumers Want?" www.atkearney.com

[19] "Foreign Direct Investment Confidence Index 2014," www.atkearney.com.

[20] Kevin Roberts, "Winning in a VUCA World", www.saatchikevin.com

[21] Michael E. Porter and Mark R. Kramer. "Creating Shared Value", Harvard Business Review 89, no. 1/2 (2011): 62-77

[22] Australian government, "Australia in the Asian Century," October 2012

[23] International Monetary Fund, World Economic Outlook database, April 2014

[24] Organisation for Economic Co-operation and Development, International Migration Database, accessed 1 September 2014

[25] Australian government, "Australia in the Asian Century" October 2012

[26] Australian government, Department of Foreign Affairs and Trade

[27] A.T. Kearney, "Ready for Takeoff: The 2014 A.T. Kearney Foreign Direct Investment Confidence Index®"

[28] IAG, "IAG Reports Strong FY14 Operating Performance and Increased Dividend", 19 August 2014

[29] Organisation for Economic Co-operation and Development, Economic Outlook for Southeast Asia, China and India 2014: Beyond the Middle-Income Trap, 2013; Lee Hsien Loong, "Scenarios for Asia in the Next 20 Years" speech at the Nikkei Conference, Tokyo, 22 May 2014

[30] Bruce Gosper, "A New Global Food Market: Trends and Opportunities for Australia" speech to Global Access Partners

Annual Growth Summit, Sydney 19 September 2013

[31] Rachael Boon, "Aesop's Tale of Expansion in Asia" *The Straits Times*, 2 September 2013; Kathy Chu, "Aesop Sees Growth From Asia, South America", *The Wall Street Journal*, 21 October 2013

[32] Homi Kharas, "The Emerging Middle Class in Developing Countries", OECD Development Centre Working Papers no. 285, 26 January 2010; United Nations Department of Economic and Social Affairs, Population Division, World Population Prospects: The 2012 Revision; United Nations Department of Economic and Social Affairs, Population Division, World Urbanization Prospects: The 2014 Revision

[33] Rebecca Thurlow, "Australia's Seek to Buy JobStreet in $524 Million Deal; Online Job Ads Firm Continues Push into Asia"; *The Wall Street Journal*, 19 February 2014

[34] David Ellis, "ANZ's Asian Growth Aspirations Make It an Interesting Alternative to Slower-Growing Domestic Banks", Morningstar, 31 July 2014

[35] "Korea's E-Government Development Amazes the World in Winning UN E-Government Survey 2012", *Korea IT Times*, 8 March 2012

[36] Hugh Thomas, "Measuring Progress Toward a Cashless Society", MasterCard Advisors, 2013

[37] Sam Grobart, "Samsung's Year Abroad", *Businessweek*, 4 April 2013

[38] Michael E. Porter and Mark R. Kramer. "Creating Shared Value", Harvard Business Review 89, no. 1/2 (2011): 62-77

[39] Ibid., p. 66

[40] 2014 Edelman Trust Barometer

[41] Responsible Investment Association Australasia, "2013 Responsible Investment Benchmark Report"

[42] Coles website, accessed 09/09/14

[43] Michael E. Porter and Mark R. Kramer, "Creating Shared Value", *Harvard Business Review* 89, no. 1/2 (2011): 62-77

[44] Social Traders, "Australian social enterprise facts", accessed 9 September 2014

[45] ASX 100 data for 1994 and 2013

[46] Arie De Geus, "The Living Company", *Harvard Business Review*, March 1997

[47] Anita M. McGahan, "How Industries Change", *Harvard Business Review*, October 2004

[48] Bridget van Kralingen, "IBM's Transformation: From Survival to Success",*Forbes*, 7 July 2010

[49] Ibid.

[50] "Selling Grindlays in India was a mistake: ANZ Chief". *Hindustan Times*, 15 August 2012

[51] "A Reign of Error", *The Sydney Morning Herald*, 2 February 2007

[52] Esther Dyson, "Netscape's Secret Weapon", *Wired*

[53] Elaine Johnson, "Kodak Facing Big Challenges in Bid to Change—Slowing of Photo Business Forces Firm to Look Elsewhere", *The Wall Street Journal*, 22 May 1985

[54] "Organisational agility: How business can survive and thrive in turbulent times", Economist Intelligence Unit, March 2009

[55] Australia has a risk aversion coefficient of -0.78, according to Natixis Economic Research (24 January 2014, no. 65)

[56] "Risk Attitudes, Development, and Growth: Experiments in 30 Countries", WZB Berlin Social Science Center, November 2013

[57] "From Purpose to Impact", Nick Craig and Scott Snook, *Harvard Business Review*, May 2014

[58] *The Five Most Important Questions You Will Ever Ask About Your Organization*, Peter F Drucker (editor), Jossey-Bass, 2008

[59] Structural considerations include a variety of methods, such as organisational design, zero-based sizing, outsourcing and near-shoring or offshoring, centralisation and decentralisation, best country locator, and demand and capacity matching. Activity value analysis is a proven method to eliminate redundant and duplicative tasks, as well as "spans and layer" optimisation.

[60] Cumulative Gallup Workplace Studies, Business Case For Diversity with Inclusion

[61] DiversityInc published annual rankings on diversity; price weighted index by Samuel A. Ramirez & Company, returns based on weekly data using Bloomberg analytics.

[62] "Social Diversity and Task Performance", Philipe, Tilenquist, and Neale, London Business School, 2008

[63] International Monetary Fund, World Economic Outlook Database, April 2014

[64] Australian Productivity Commission, "Enhancing Australia's Productivity Growth", chapter 1 in *Annual Report 2007–08* (Canberra: 2008)

[65] Australian Bureau of Statistics, Australian National Accounts: National Income, Expenditure and Product, March 2014

[66] Australian Bureau of Statistics, 3222.0 Population Projections, Australia, 2012 (base) to 2101

[67] Australian Bureau of Statistics, 5260.0.55.002 – Estimates of Industry Multifactor Productivity, 2012–13

[68] Saul Eslake, "Productivity: the lost decade", Annual Policy Conference of the Reserve Bank of Australia, HC Coombs Conference Centre, Kirribilli, Sydney, vol. 15. (2011)

[69] A.T. Kearney, "Time to Tell Your CPOs to Collaborate with Suppliers", 2012

[70] Bronwyn H. Hall, "Innovation and productivity", *Innovation* (2011): 028

[71] Department of Innovation, Industry, Science and Research, *Innovation and Raising Australia's Productivity Growth*, 2011

[72] Ibid.

[73] Australian Bureau of Statistics, 8158.0 - Innovation in Australian Business, 2012-13

[74] A.T. Kearney Leadership Excellence in Analytic Practices (LEAP) survey of 430 senior executives across 10 countries and more than 11 industries

[75] A.T. Kearney retail analytics point of view

[76] A.T. Kearney LEAP Survey

[77] Frank Germann, Gary L. Lilien, and Arvind Rangaswamy, "Performance Implications of Deploying Marketing Analytics," *International Journal of Research in Marketing*, 2013

[78] Julia King, "How analytics helped Ford turn its fortunes",*CMO*, 2 December 2013

[79] Kashmir Hill, "How Target Figured Out A Teen Girl Was Pregnant Before Her Father Did", *Forbes*, 16 February 2012

[80] "Performance Implications of Deploying Marketing Analytics", Frank Germann, Gary L. Lilien, Arvind Rangaswamy, 2013

[81] Brad Howarth, "Big data analytics: The new black magic of marketing?",*CMO*, 24 October 2013

Nigel Andrade is an A.T. Kearney partner and member of the firm's Financial Institutions practice in Asia Pacific. With more than 15 years of management consulting experience, Nigel specialises in customer-led innovation, partnering with companies and organisations across Australia, Southeast Asia, India, Europe, and North America to help them unlock tangible and sustainable value. He is based in Sydney.

Peter Munro is an A.T. Kearney partner based in Sydney. Formerly the managing director of Australia and New Zealand, Peter now leads the firm's Strategy, Marketing and Sales practice in APAC. With more than 20 years of management consulting experience, he specialises in corporate and business unit strategy, strategy implementation, and operations transformation.